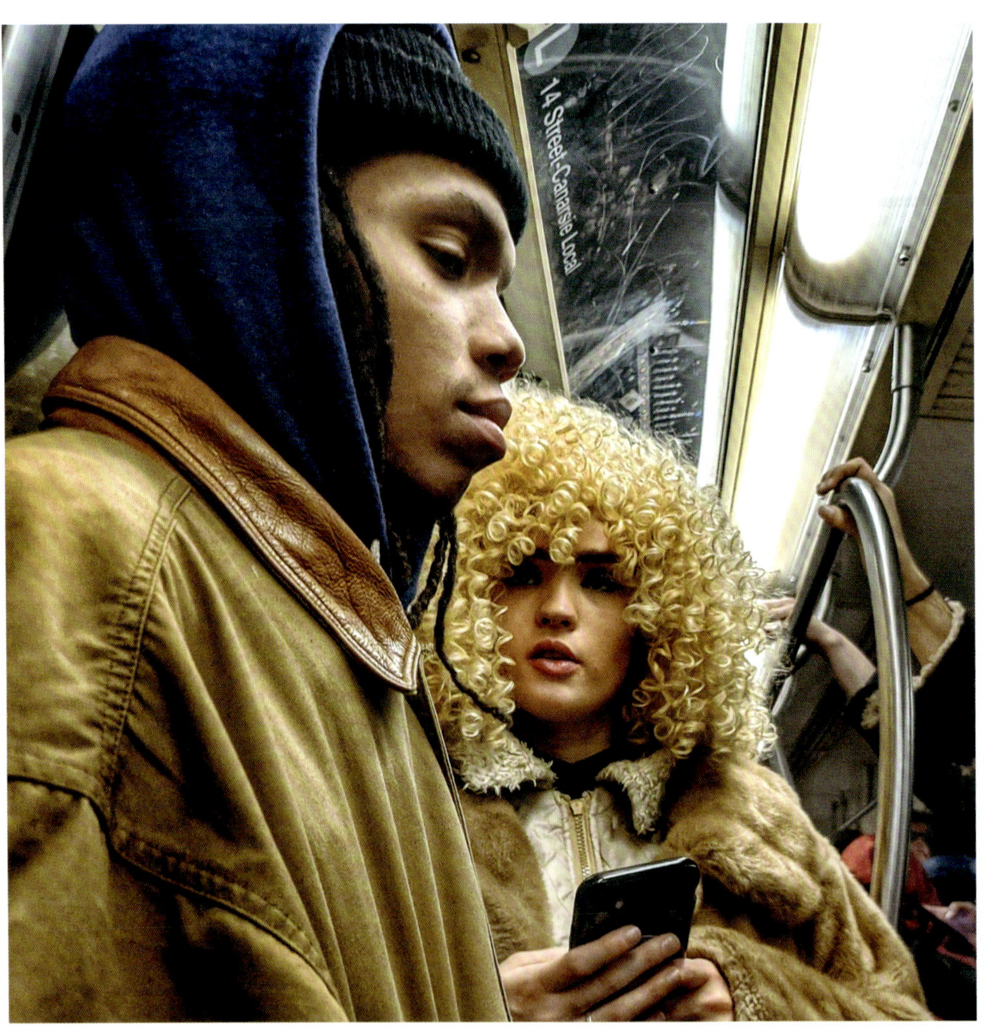

14 Street-Canarsie Local

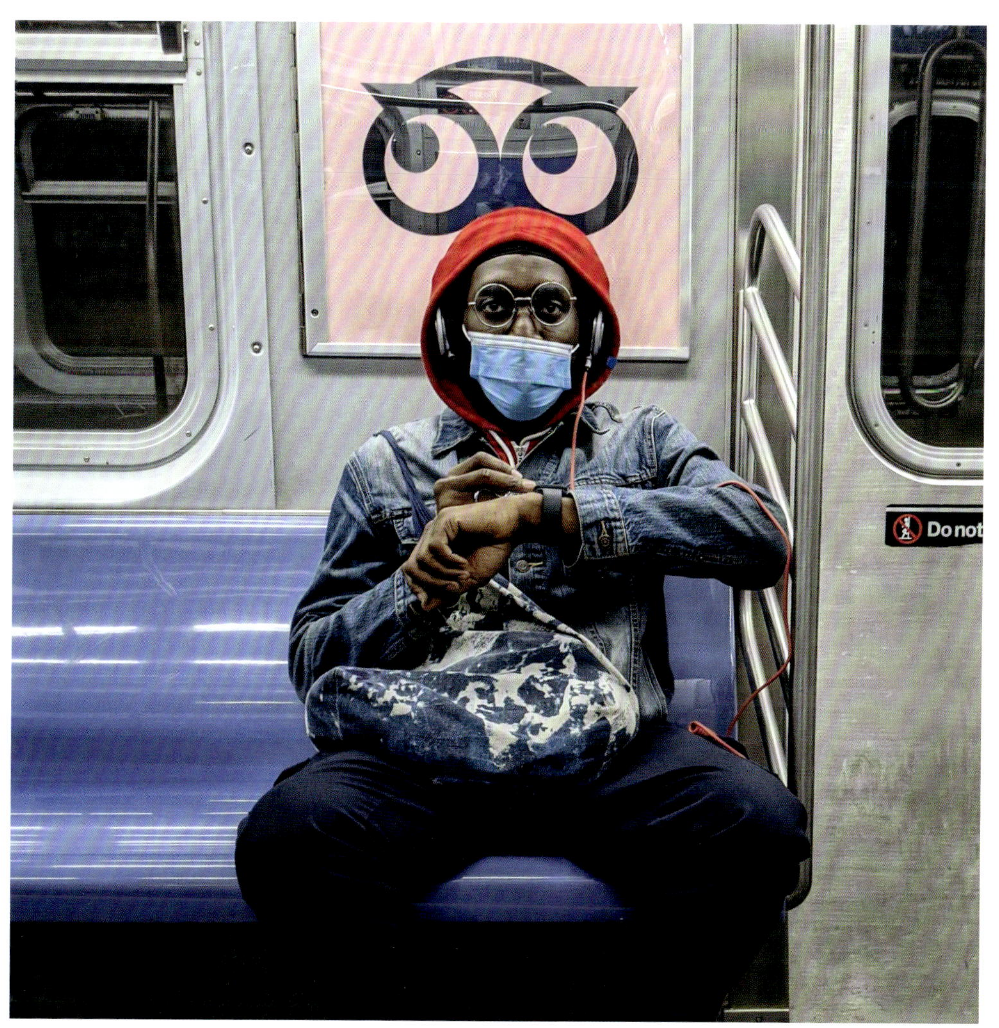

Do not

Cofounders: Taj Forer and Michael Itkoff
Creative Director: Ursula Damm
Copy Editor: Gabrielle Fastman

ISBN: 978-1-954119-15-4

Printed by Ofset Yapimevi, Turkey

Daylight Books
E-mail: info@daylightbooks.org
Web: www.daylightbooks.org

Daylight

SUBWAYGRAM

Chris Maliwat

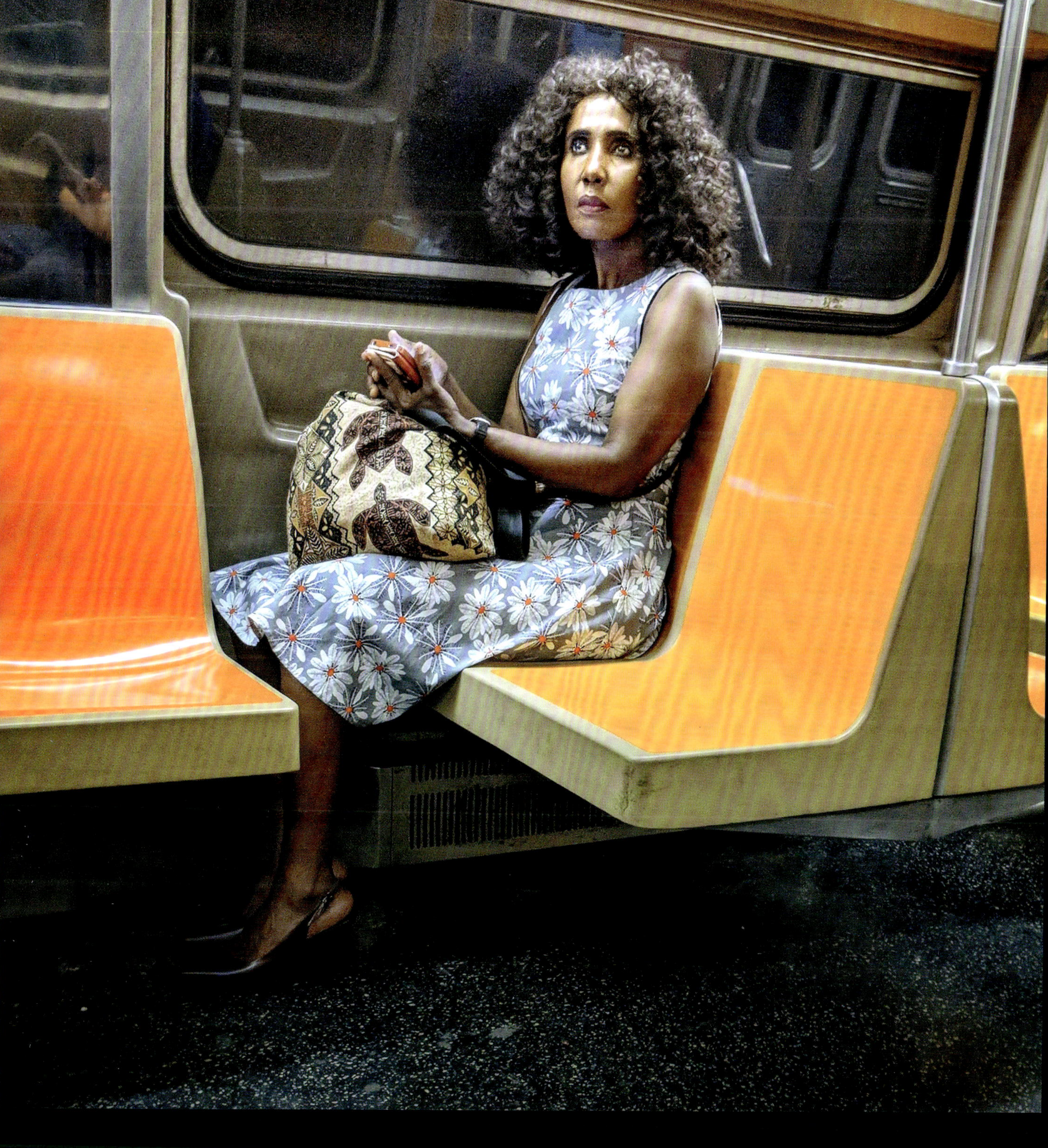

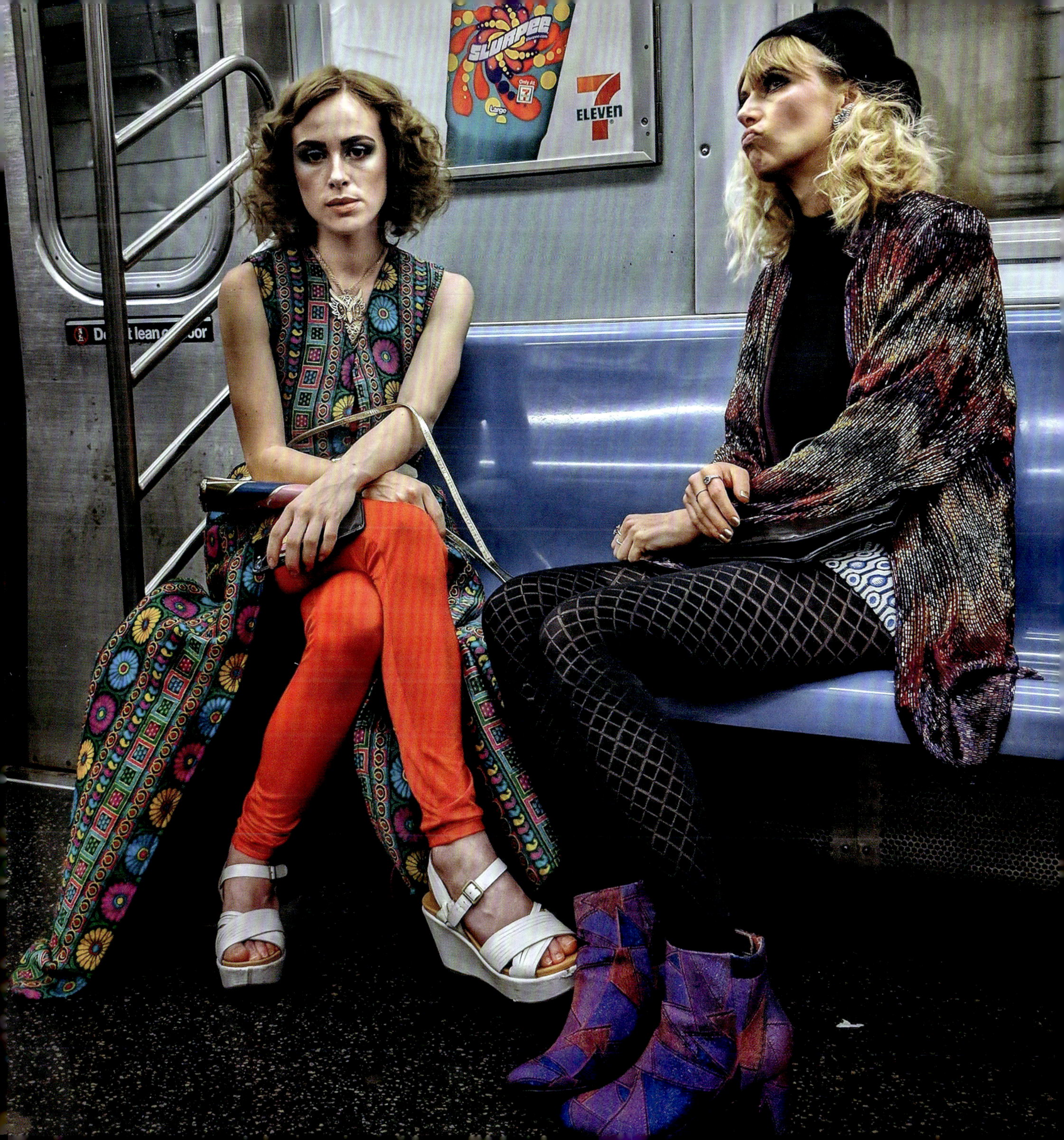

SLURPEE
slurpee.com
Only At
Large
7
ELEVEN
Do not lean on door

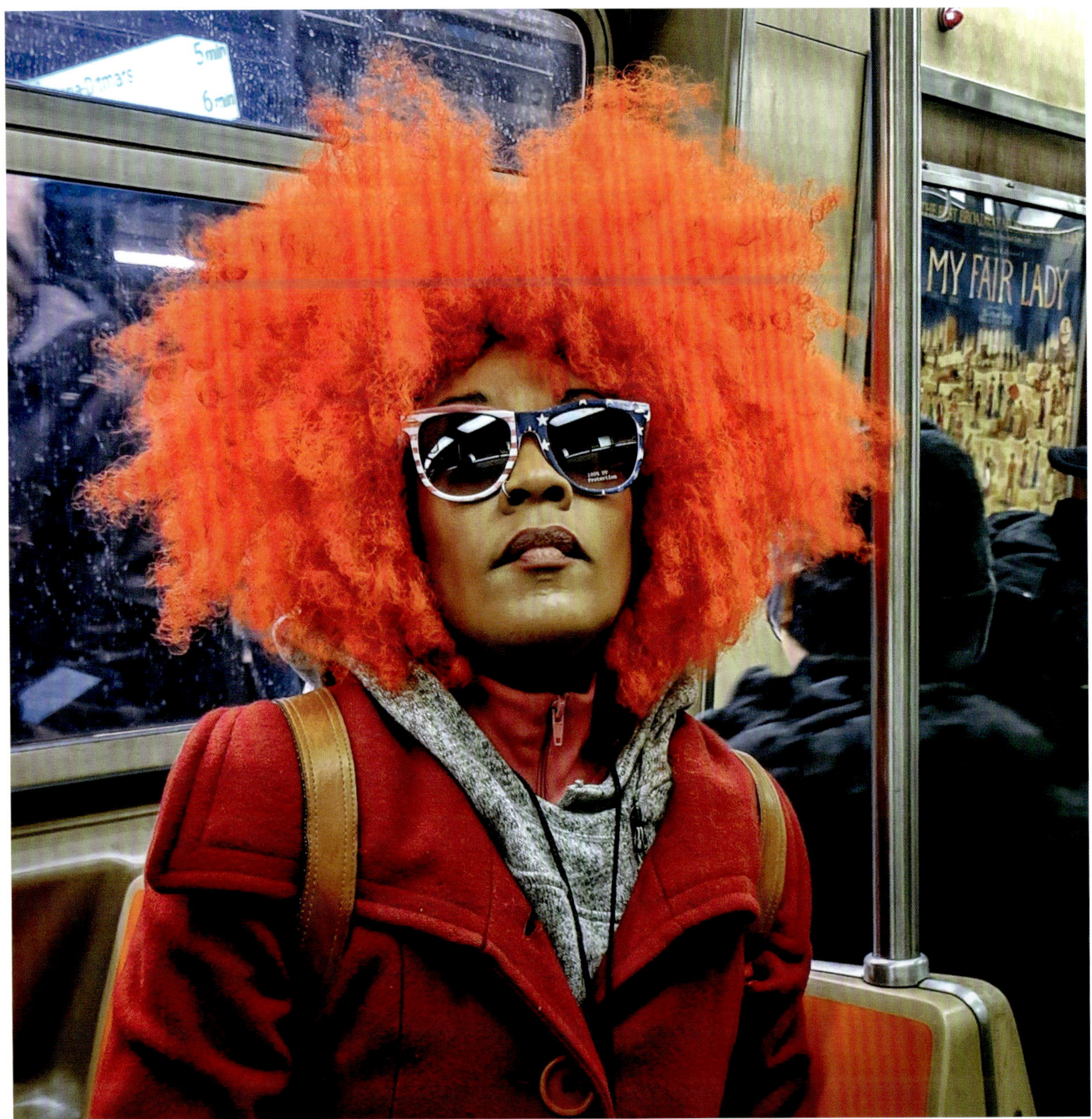
5 min
6 min
MY FAIR LADY

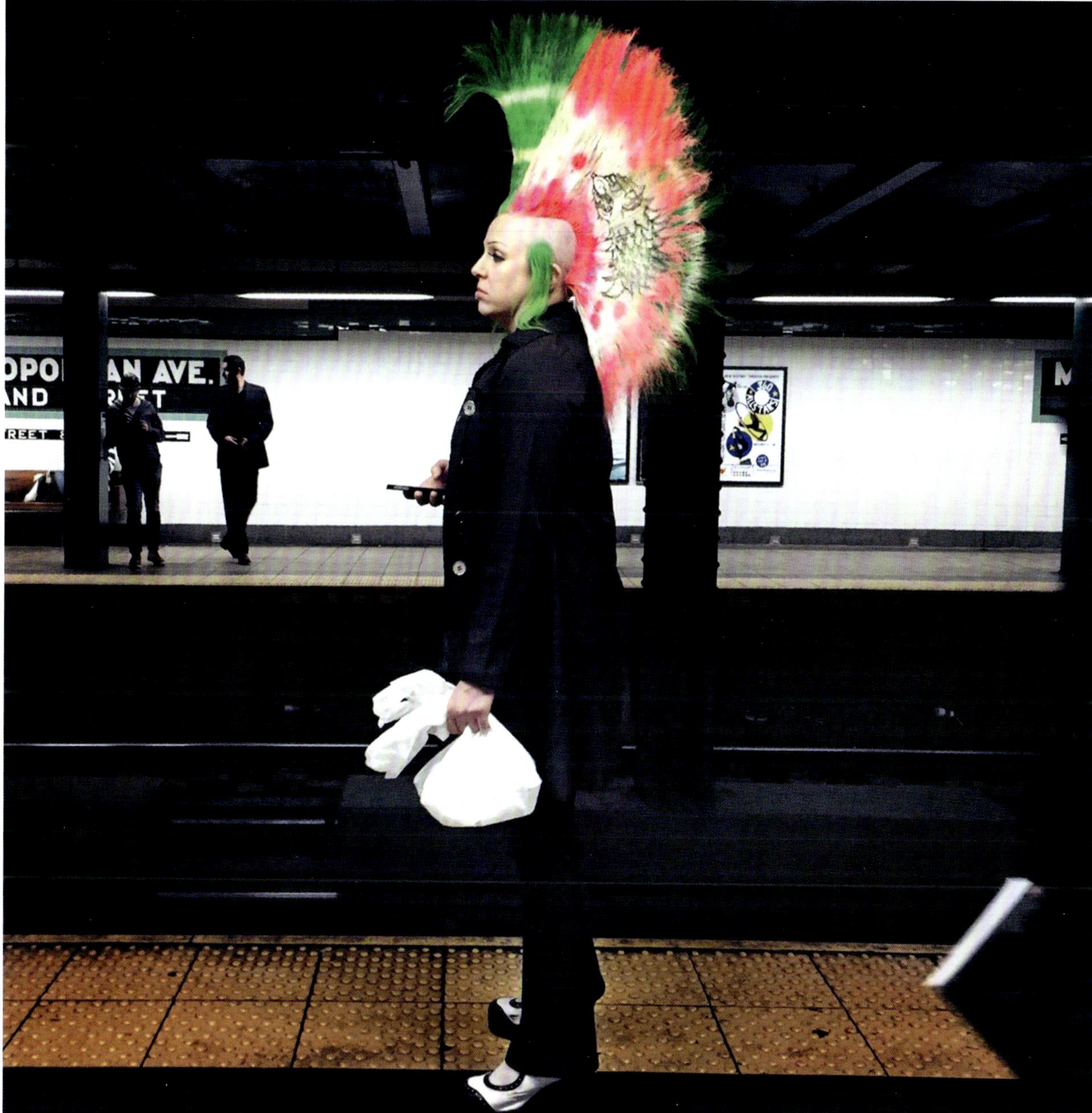
OPOL   AN AVE.
AND   REET
REET   8
M

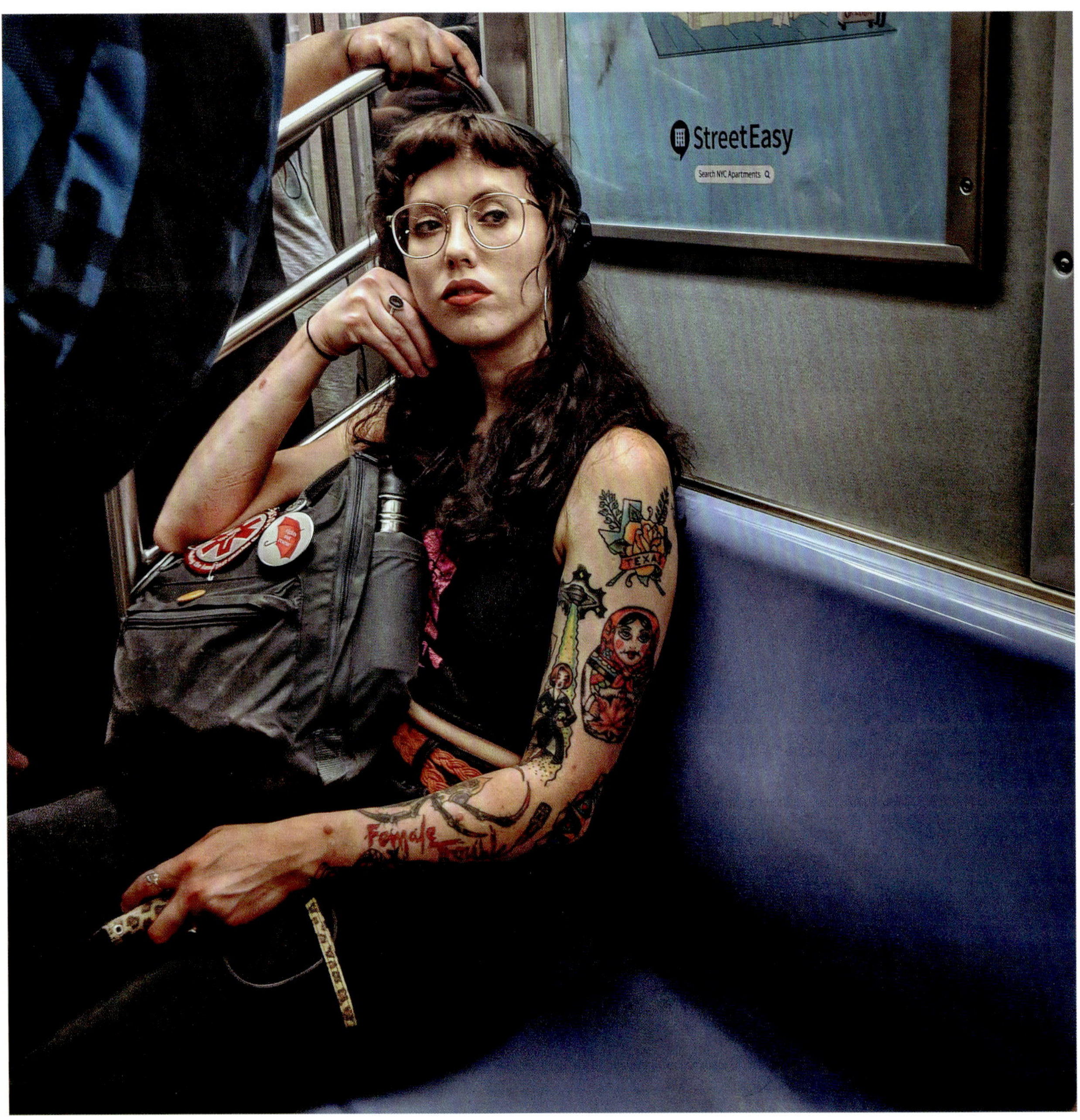
StreetEasy
Search NYC Apartments

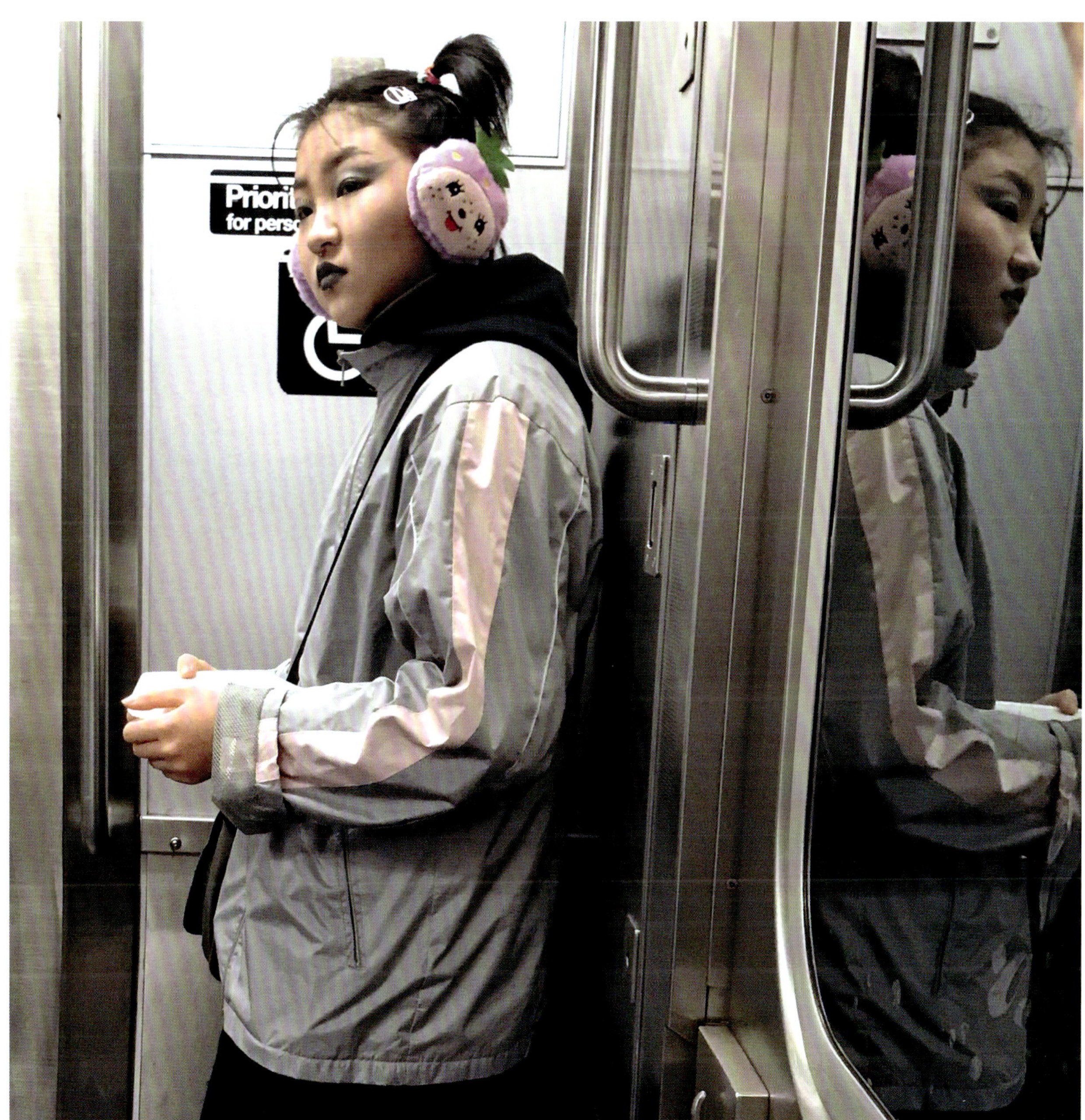
Priorit
for perso

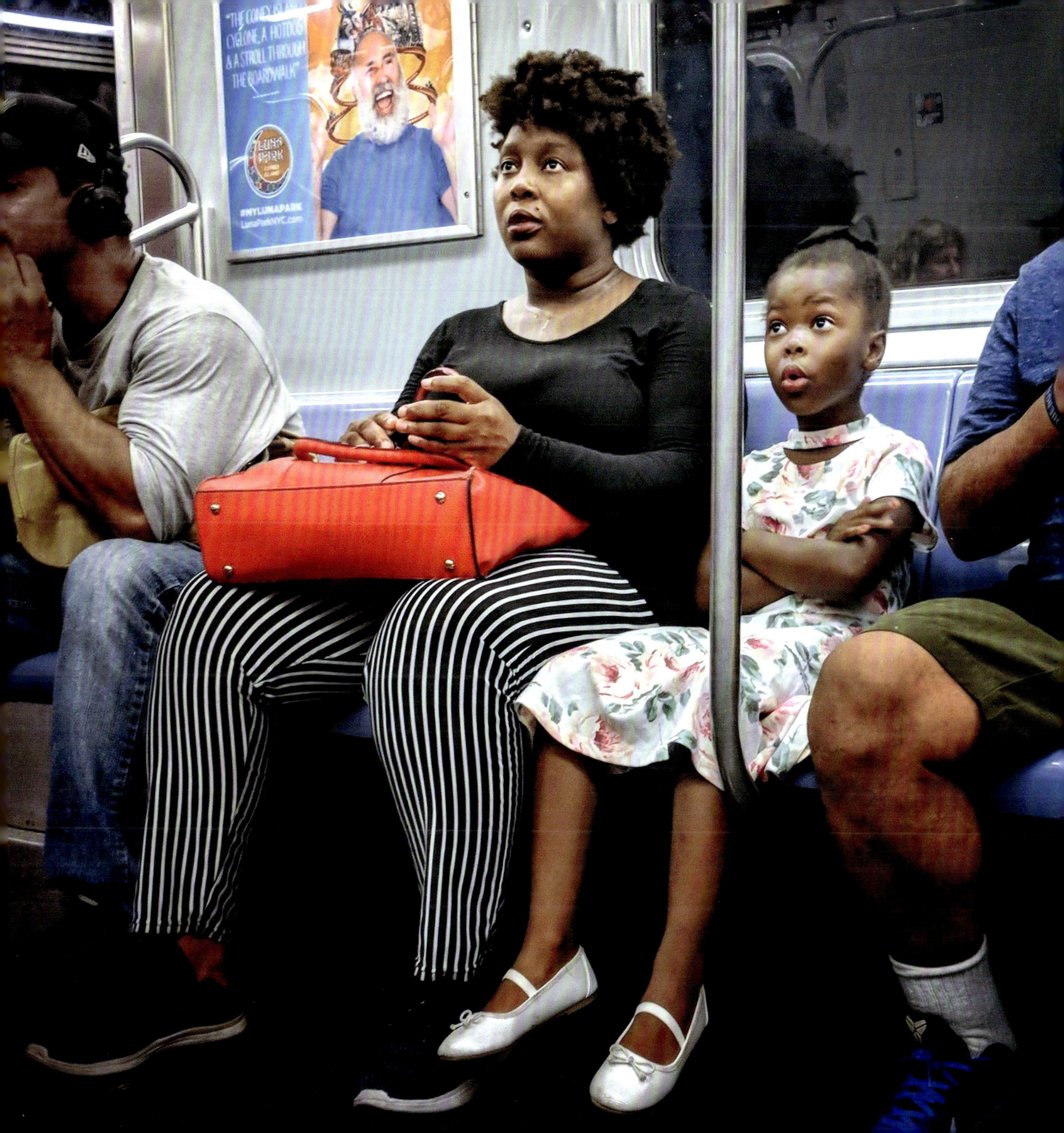

"THE CONEY ISLAND
CYCLONE, A HOTDOG
& A STROLL THROUGH
THE BOARDWALK"
LUNA PARK
#MYLUNAPARK
LunaParkNYC.com

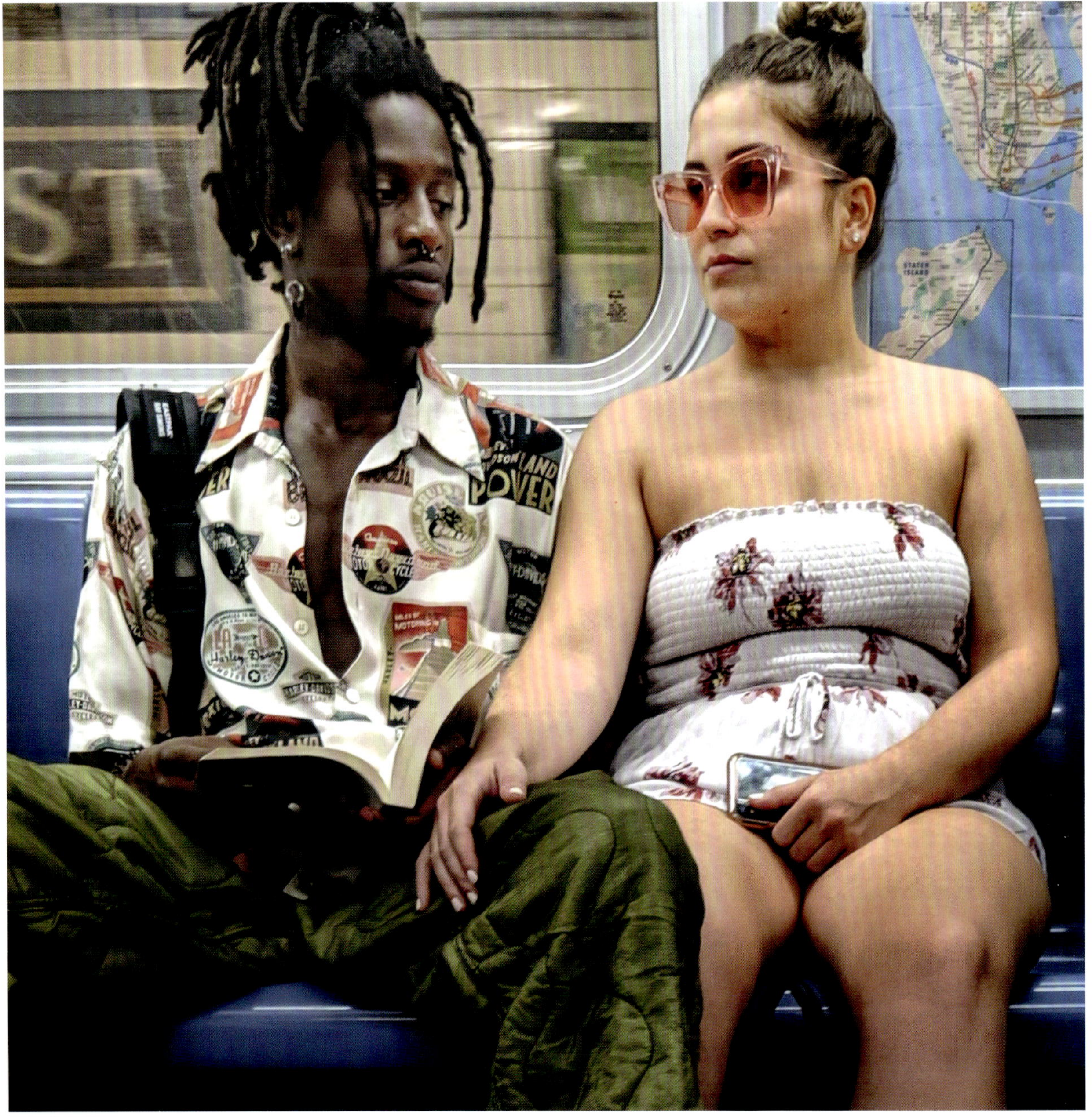

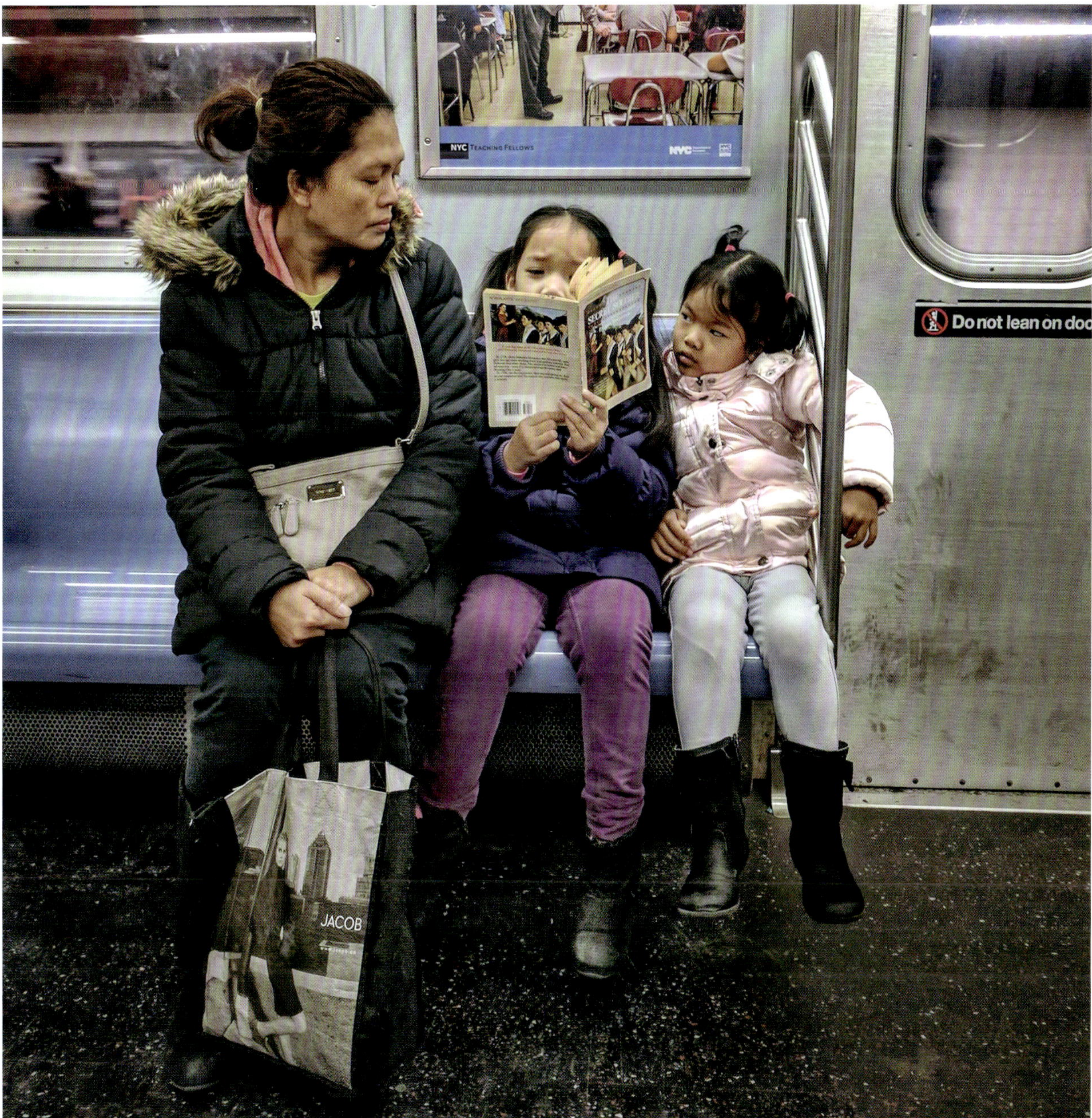

NYC TEACHING FELLOWS
NYC
Do not lean on doo
JACOB

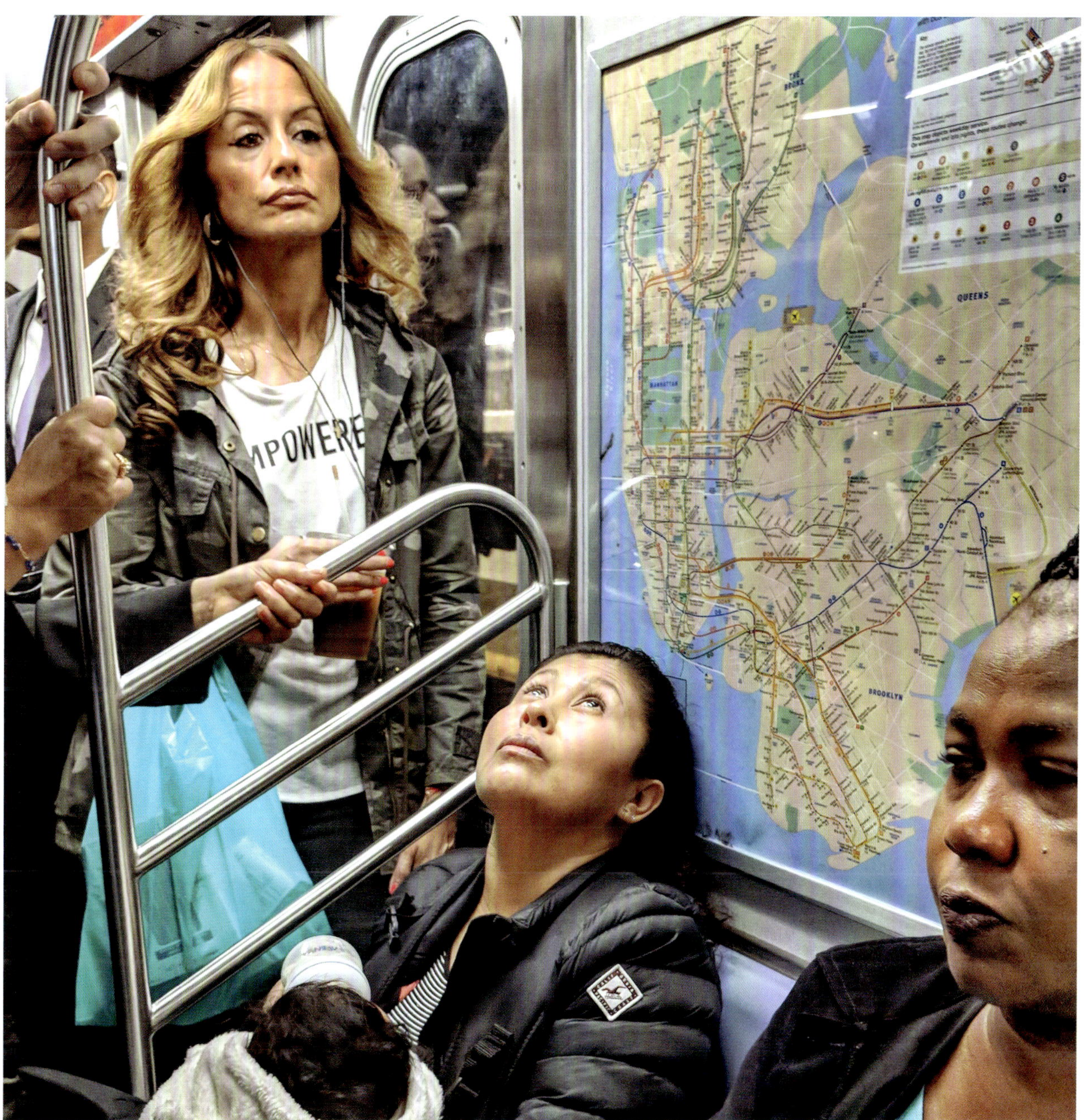

MPOWERE
THE BRONX
QUEENS
MANHATTAN
BROOKLYN

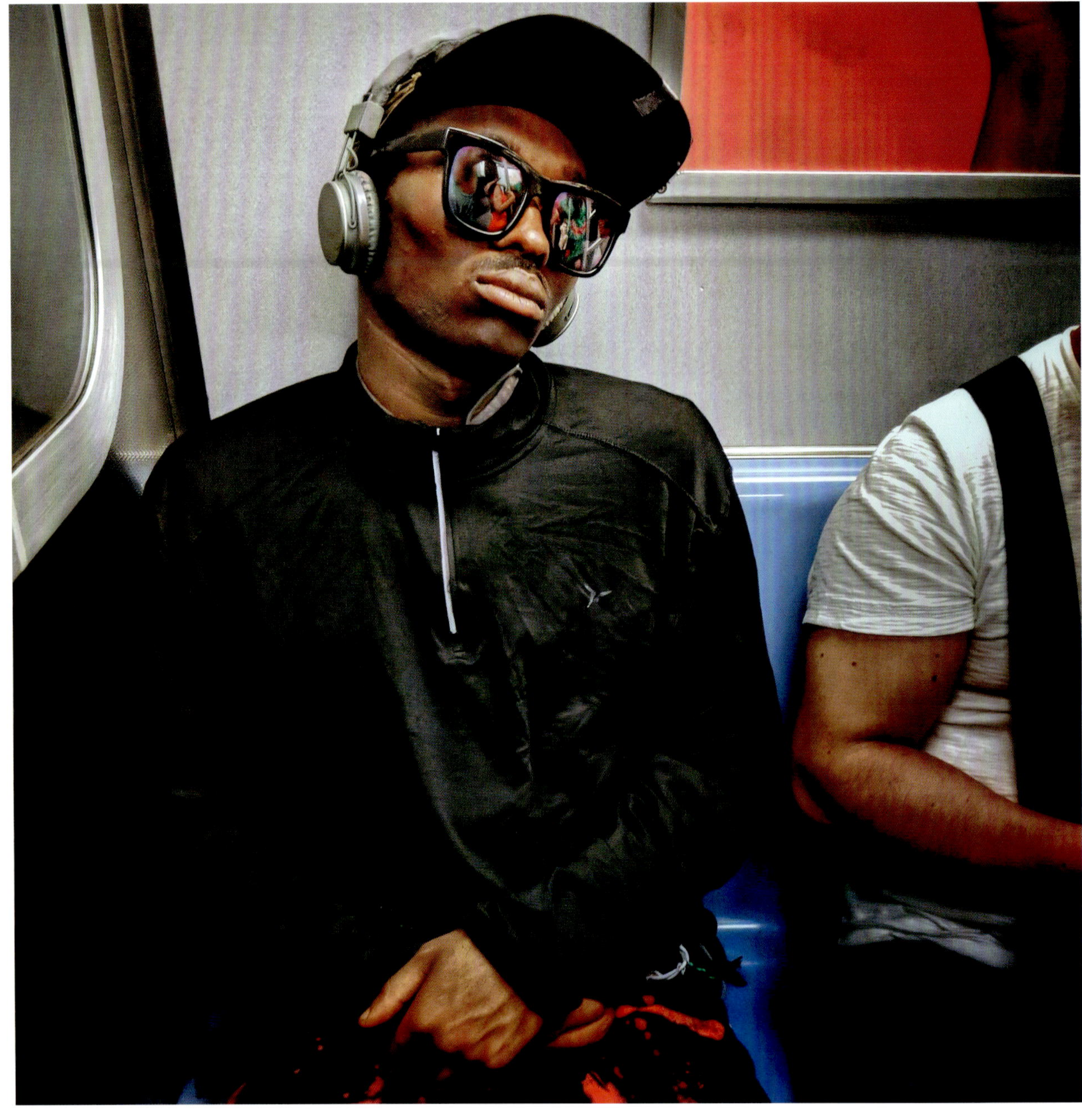

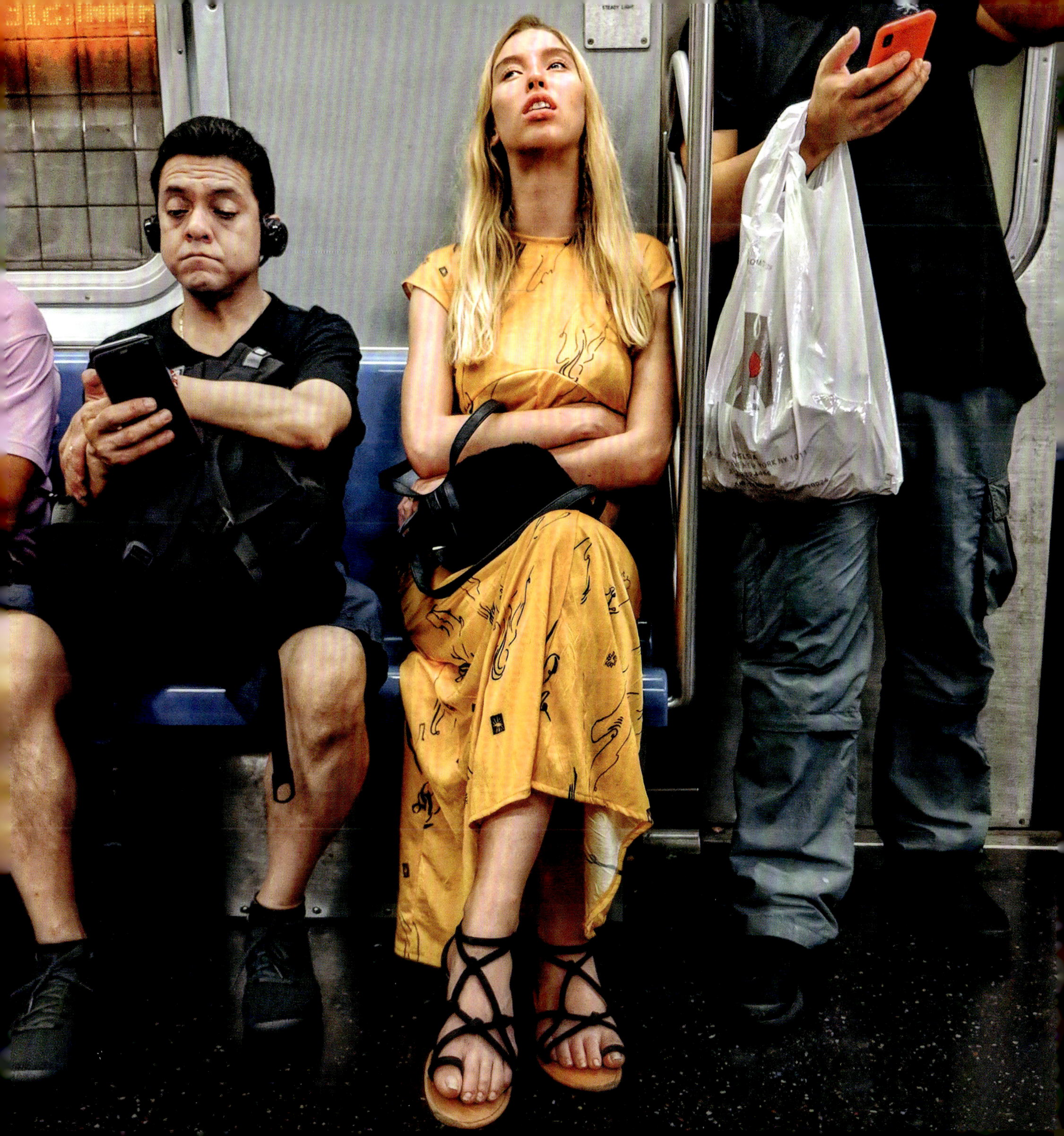

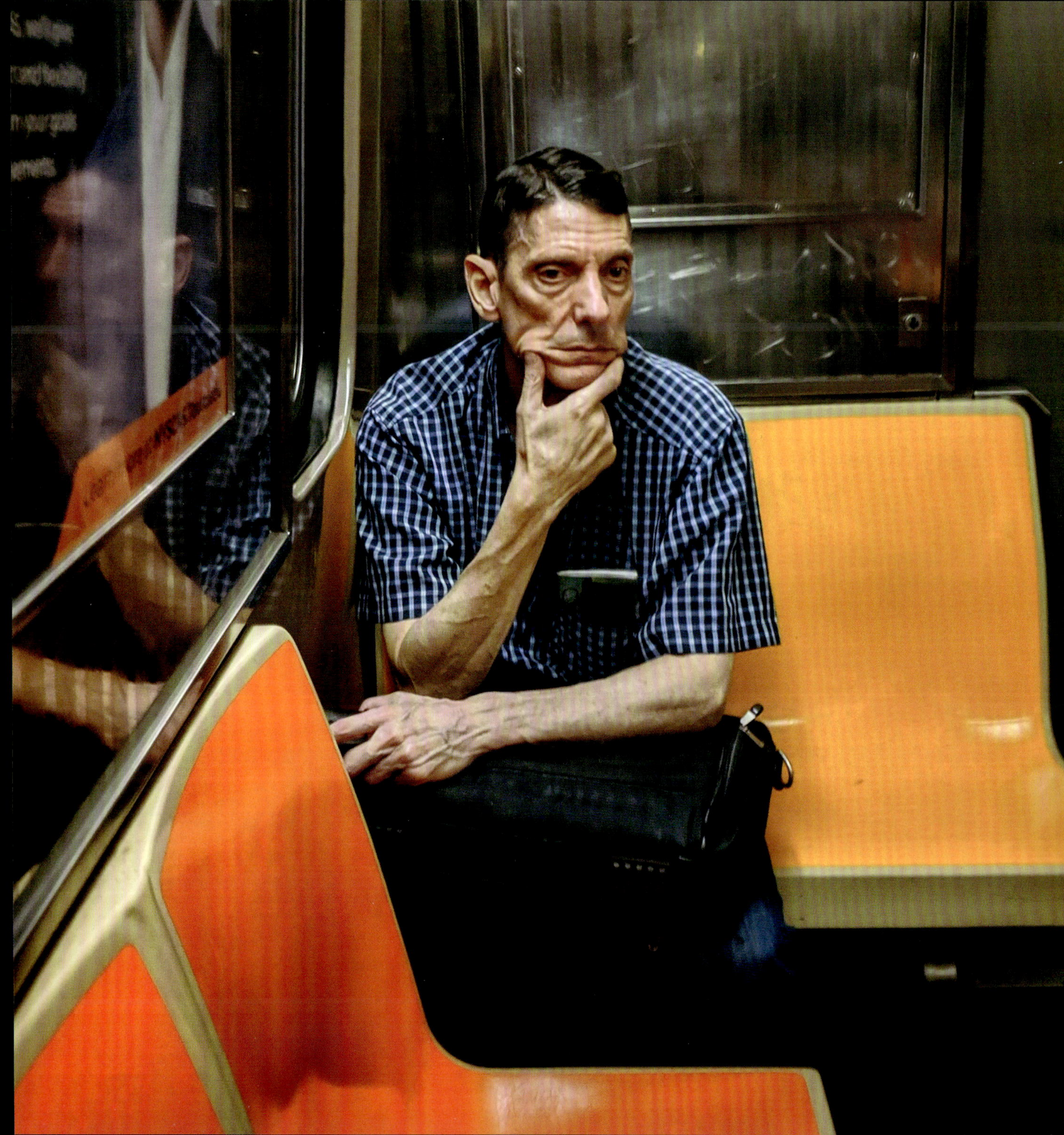

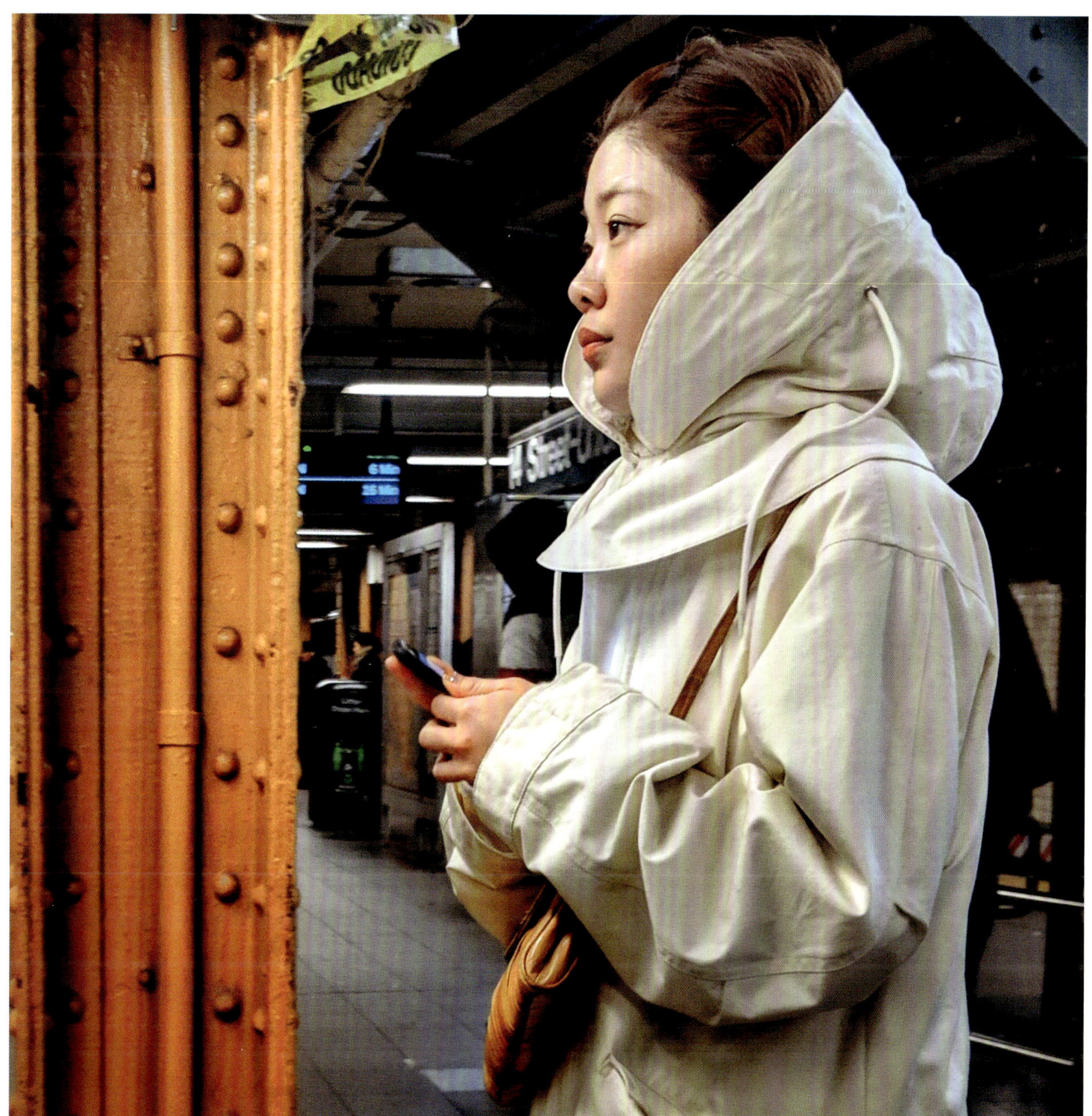

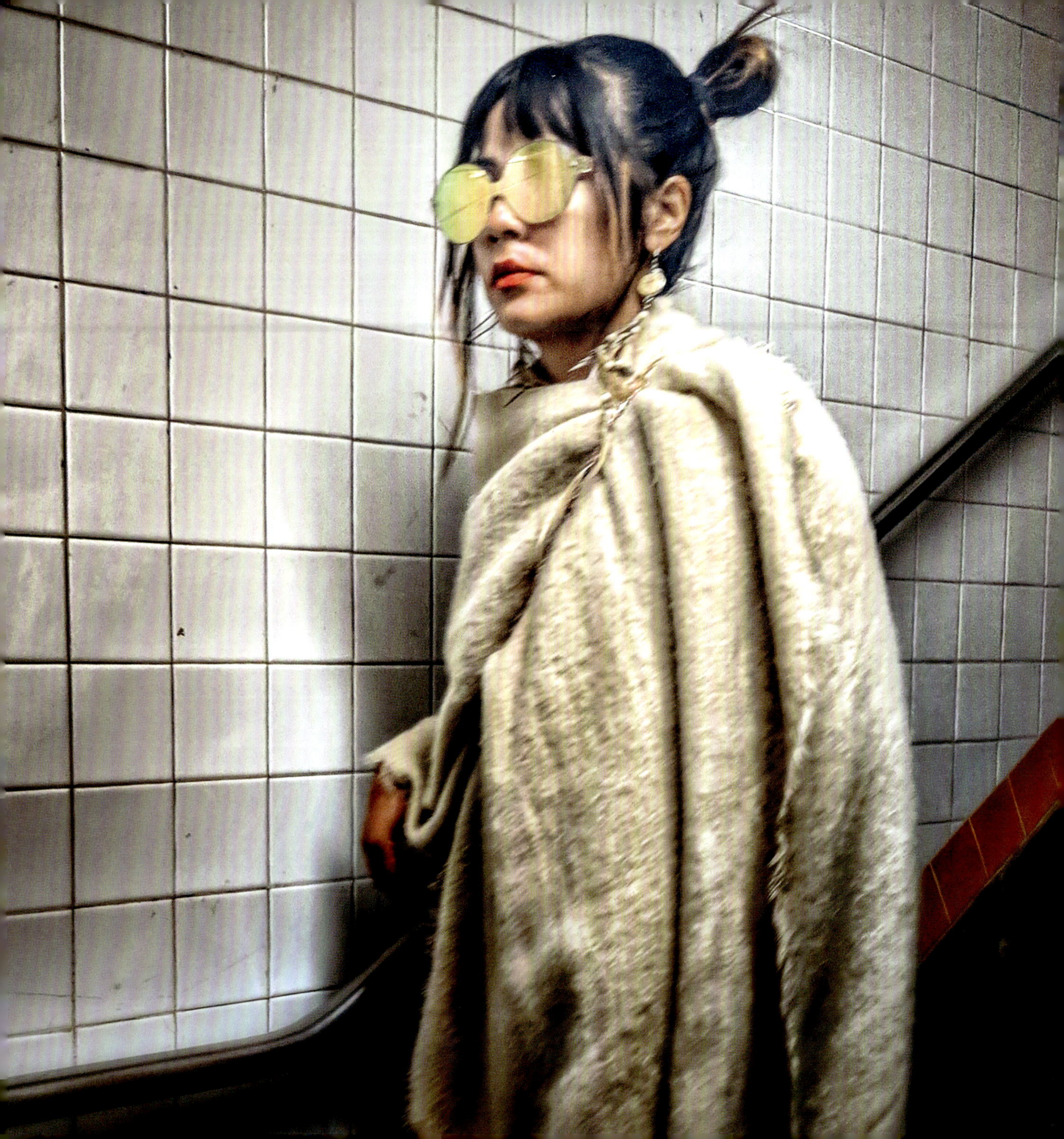

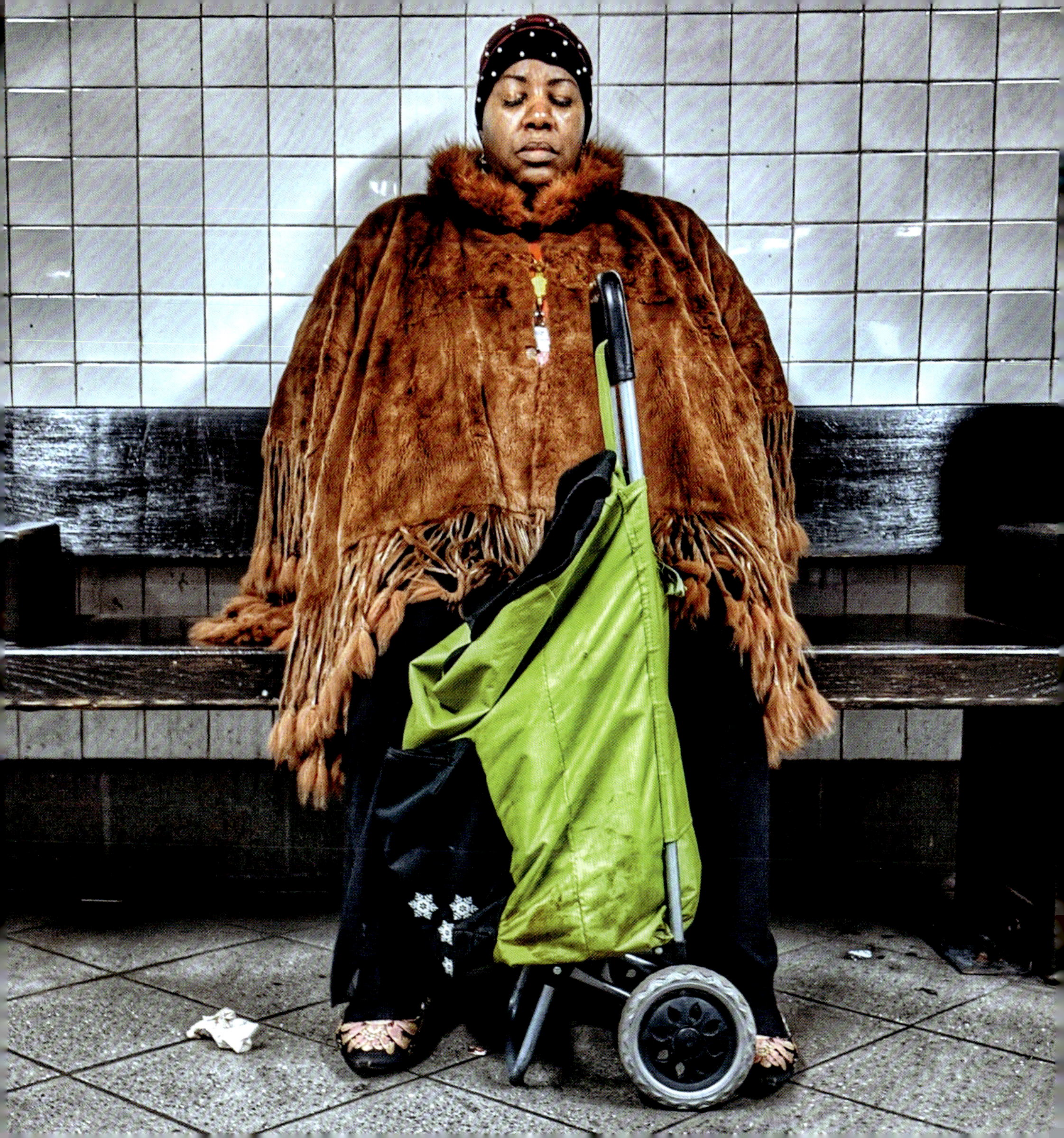

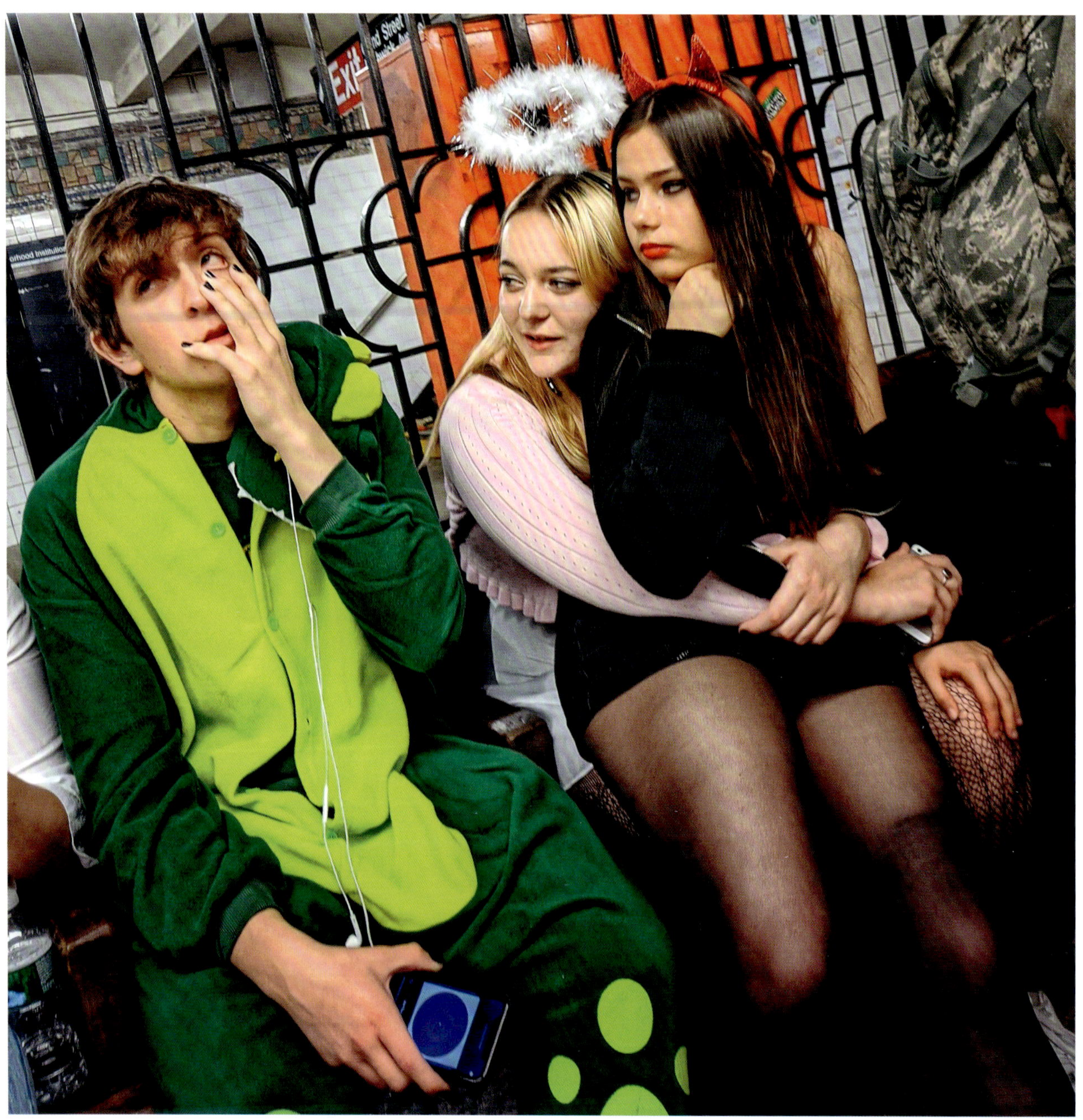

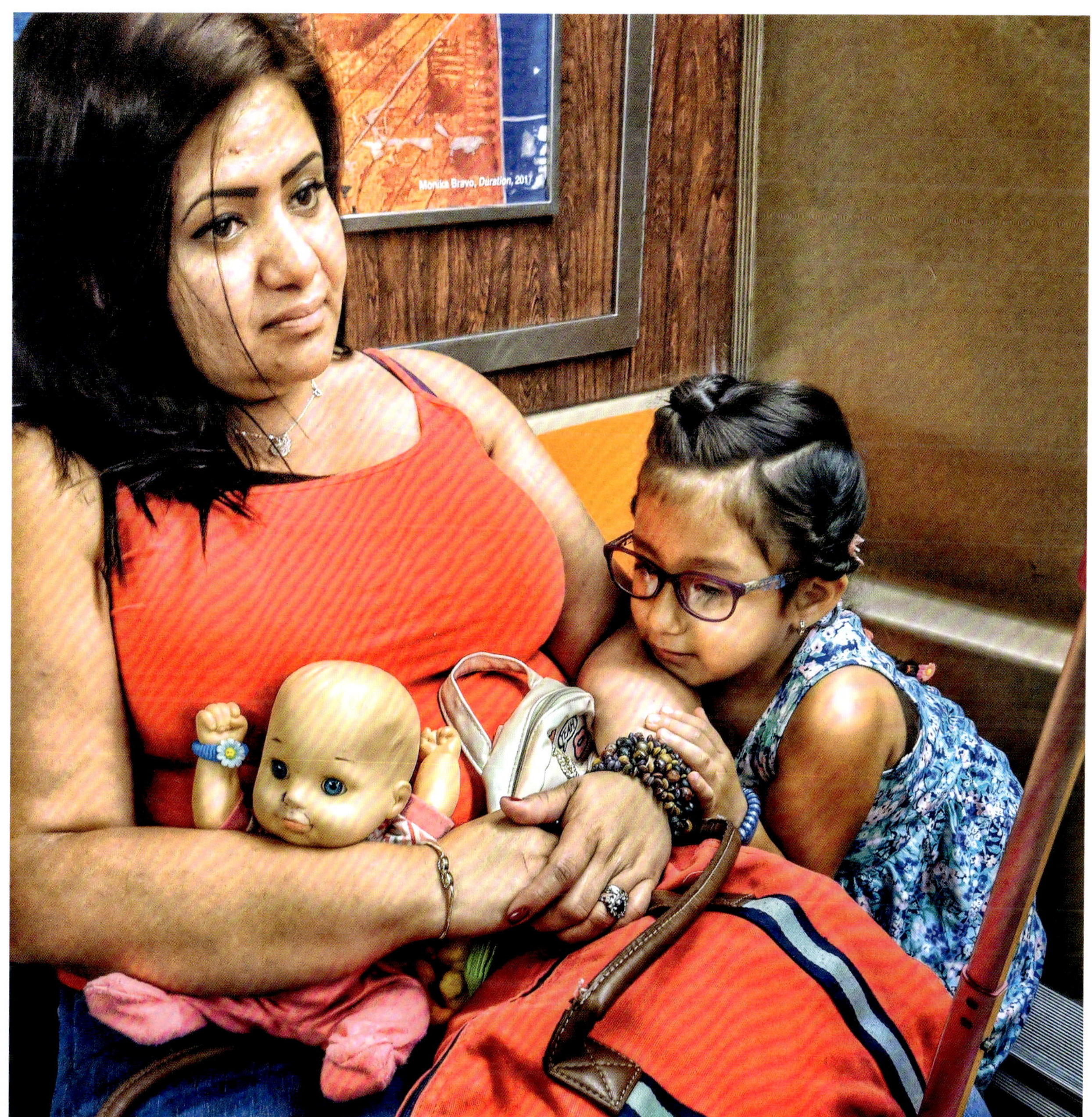

Monika Bravo, Duration, 2017

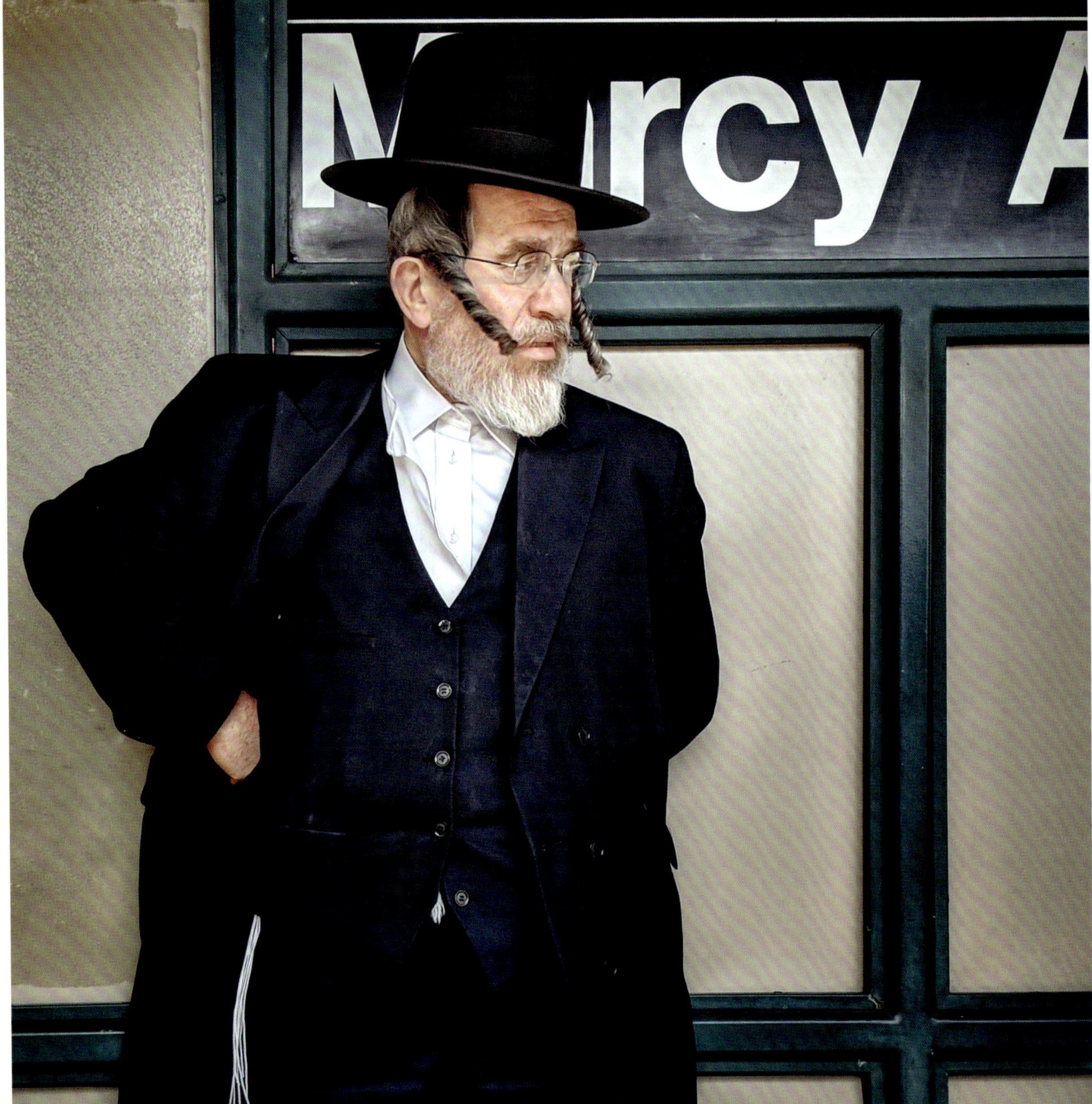

Mercy A

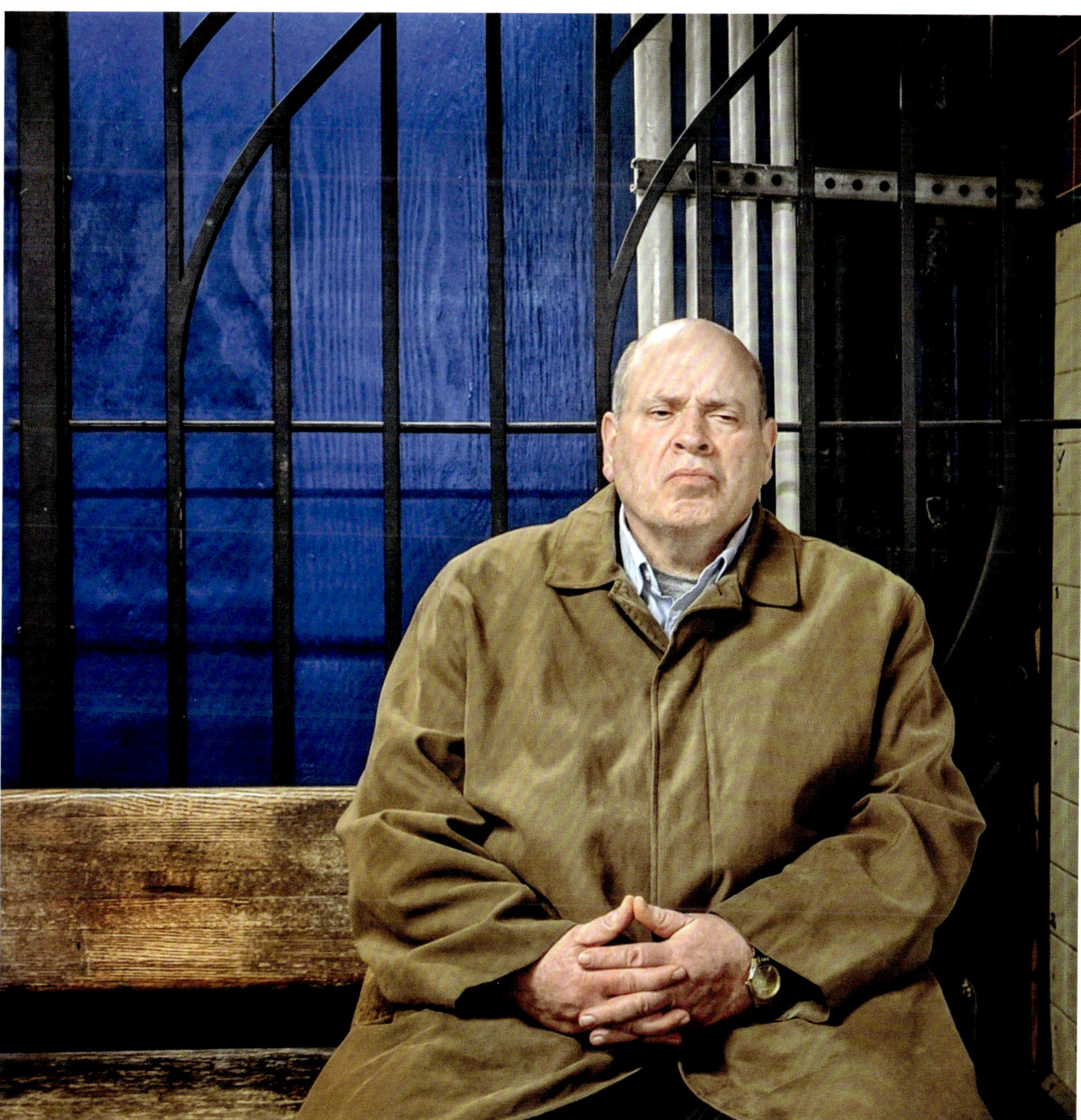

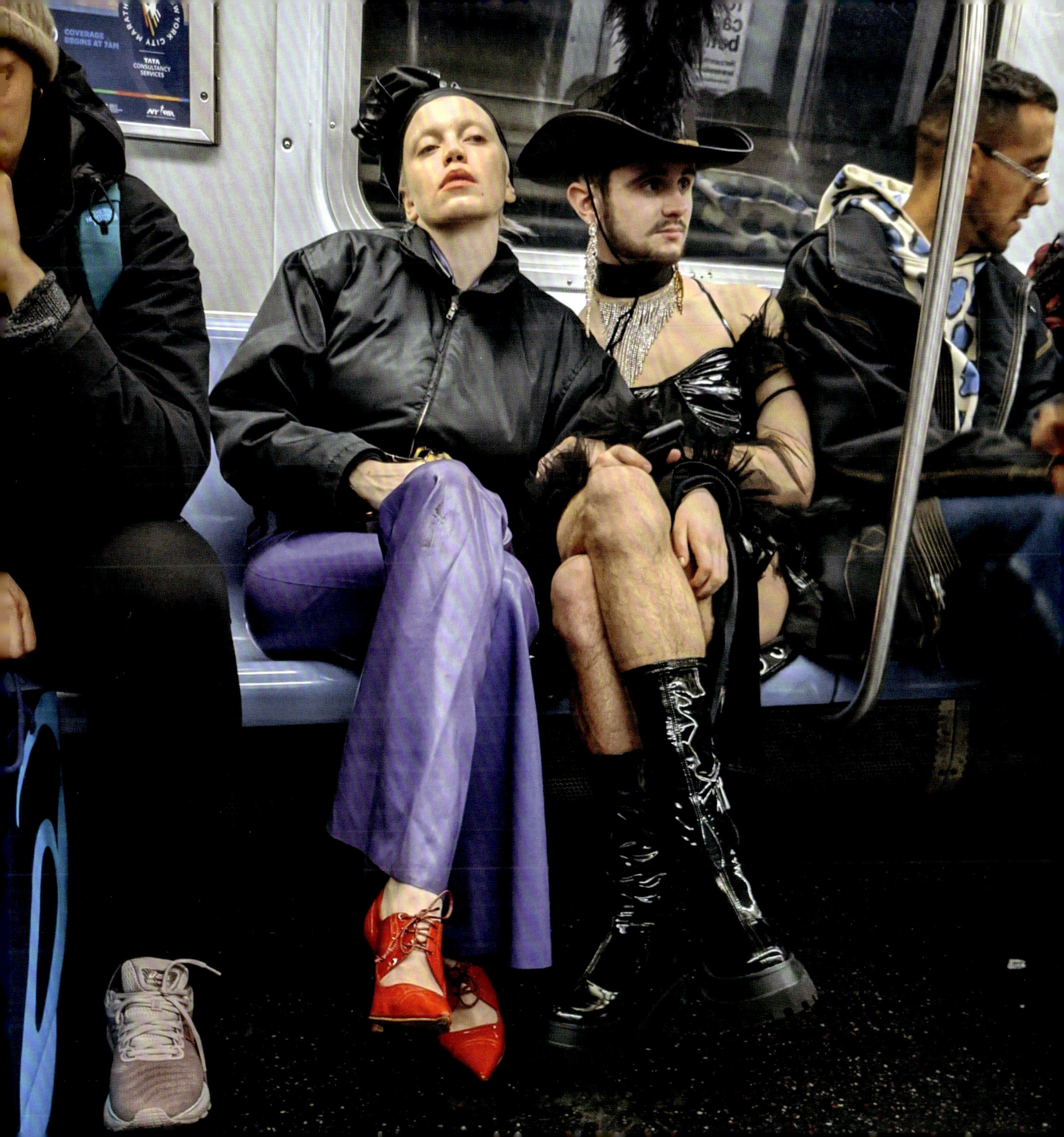

NEW YORK CITY MARATHON
COVERAGE
BEGINS AT 7AM
TATA
CONSULTANCY
SERVICES

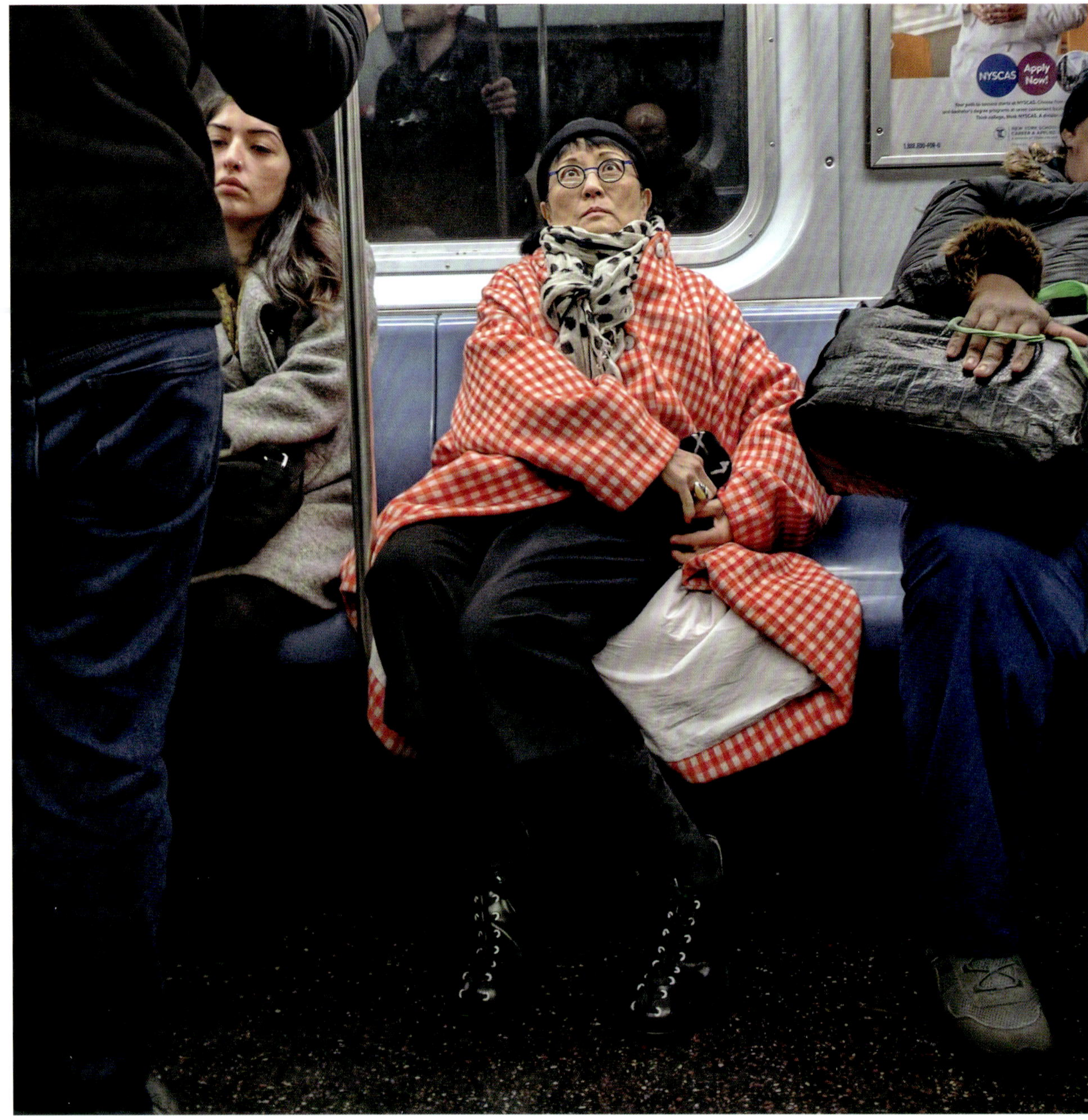

NYSCAS
Apply Now!

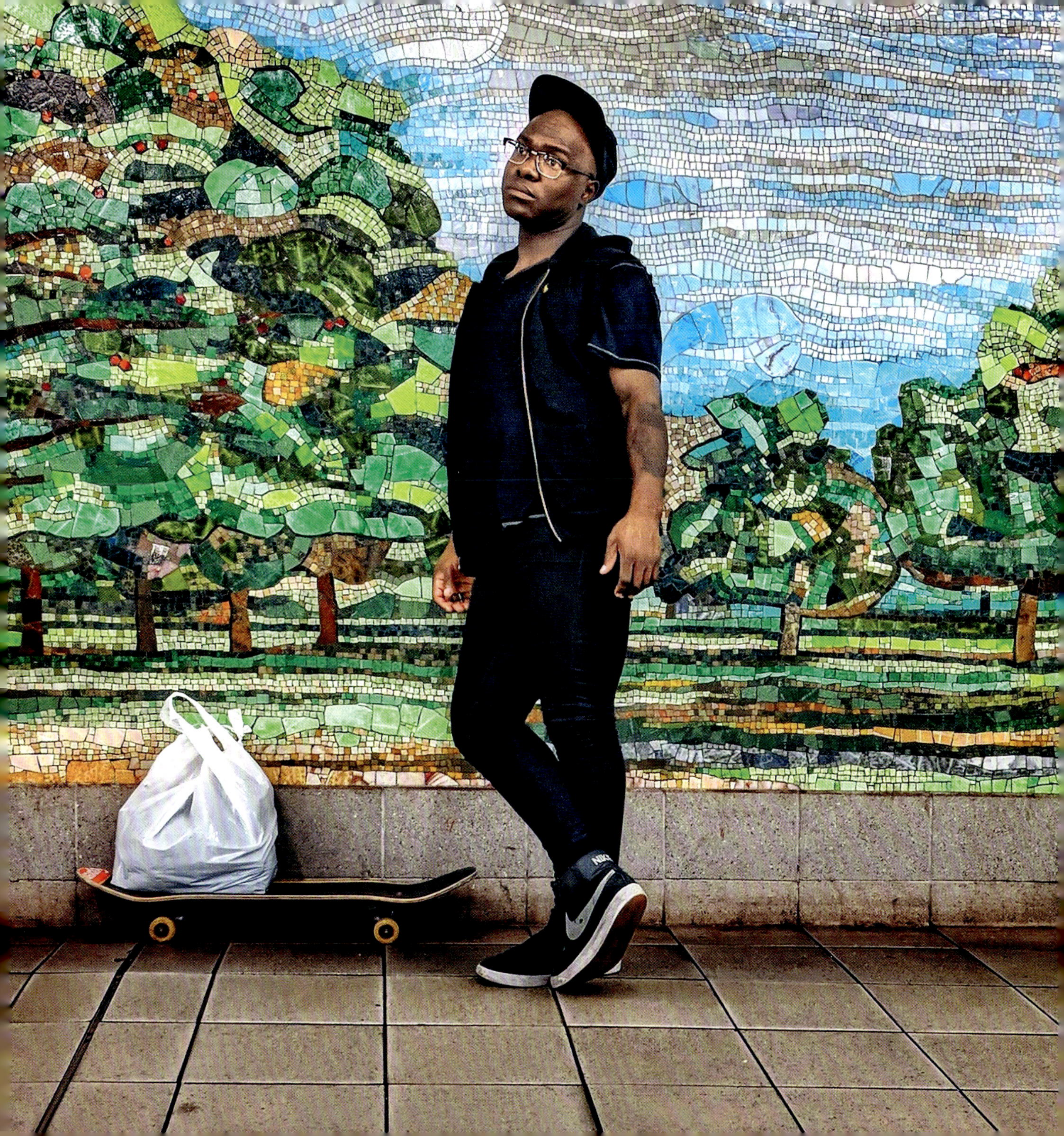

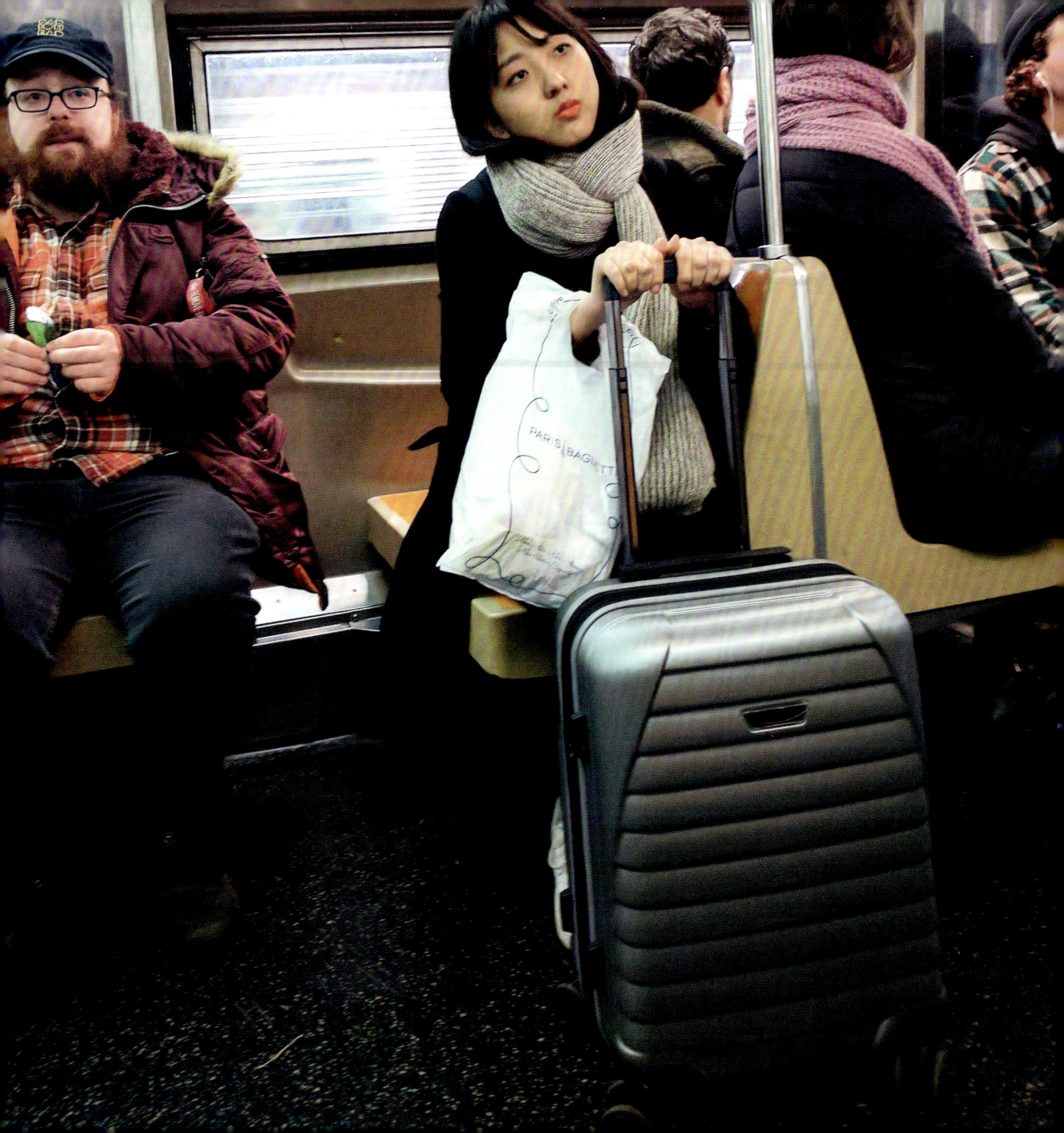

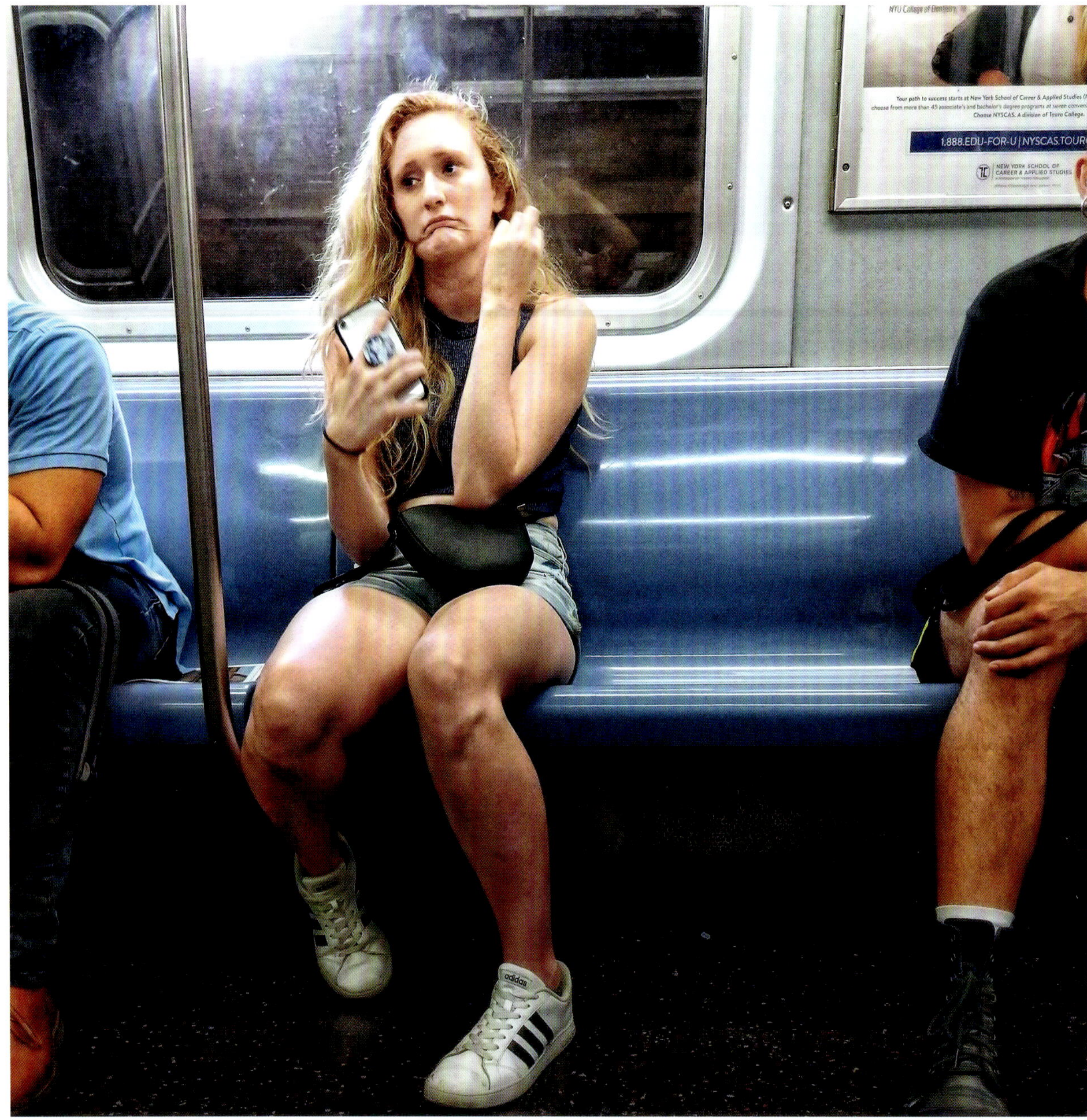

NYU College of Dentistry
Your path to success starts at New York School of Career & Applied Studies (N
choose from more than 45 associate's and bachelor's degree programs at seven conveni
Choose NYSCAS. A division of Touro College.
1.888.EDU-FOR-U | NYSCAS.TOUR
NEW YORK SCHOOL OF
CAREER & APPLIED STUDIES

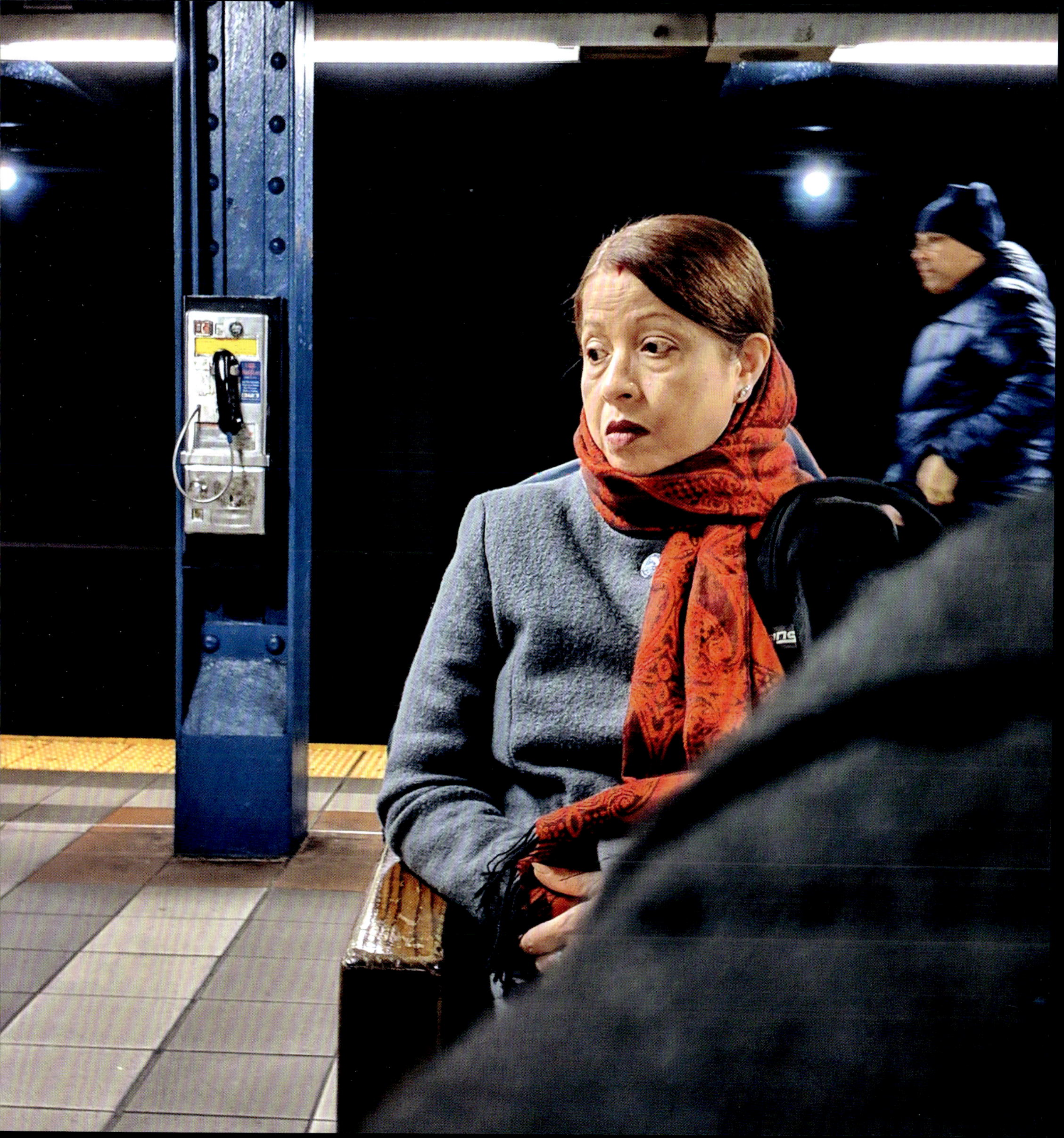

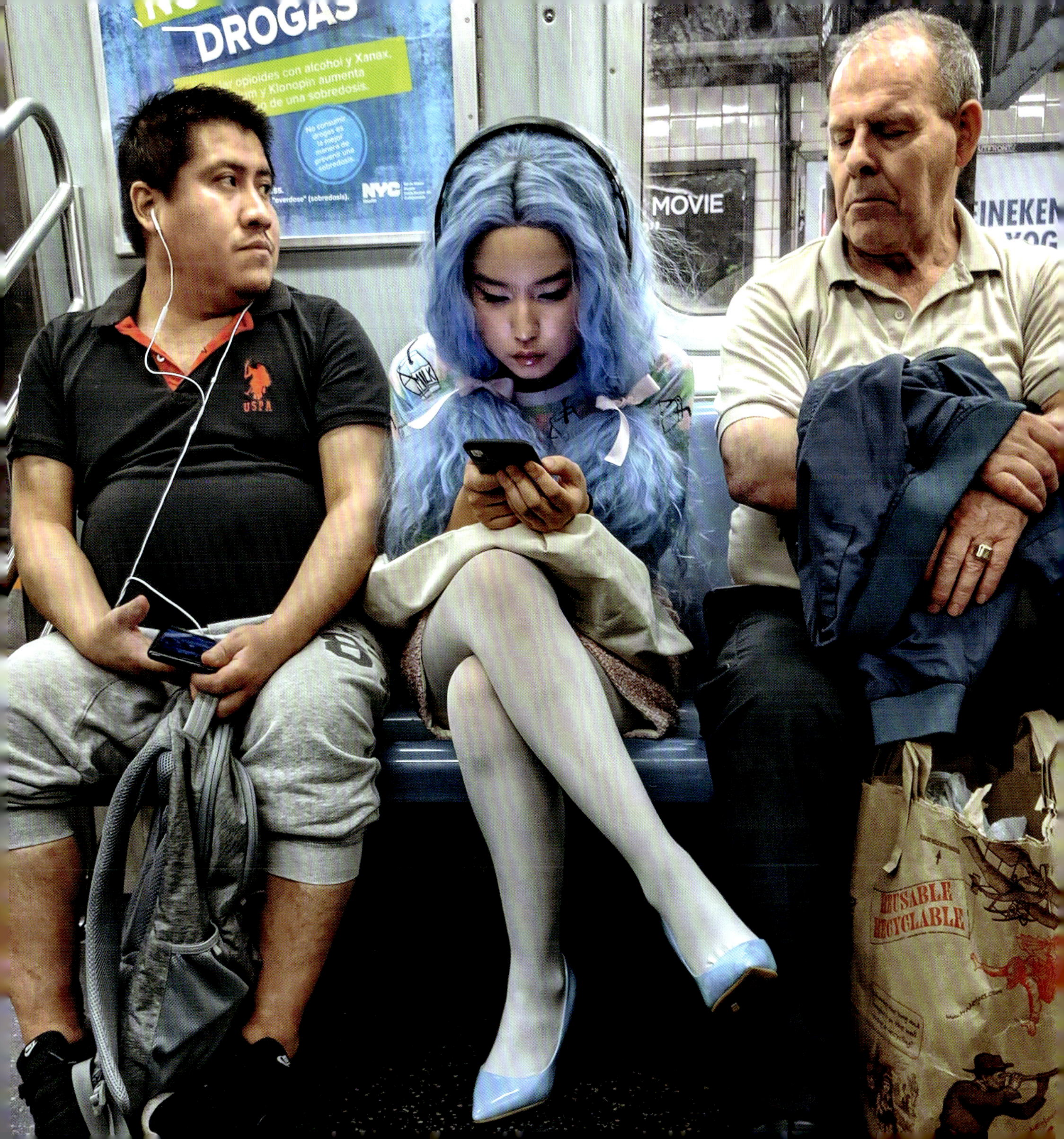
DROGAS
...lar opioides con alcohol y Xanax,
...m y Klonopin aumenta
...o de una sobredosis.
No consumir
drogas es
la mejor
manera de
prevenir una
sobredosis
"overdose" (sobredosis).
NYC
MOVIE
REUSABLE
RECYCLABLE

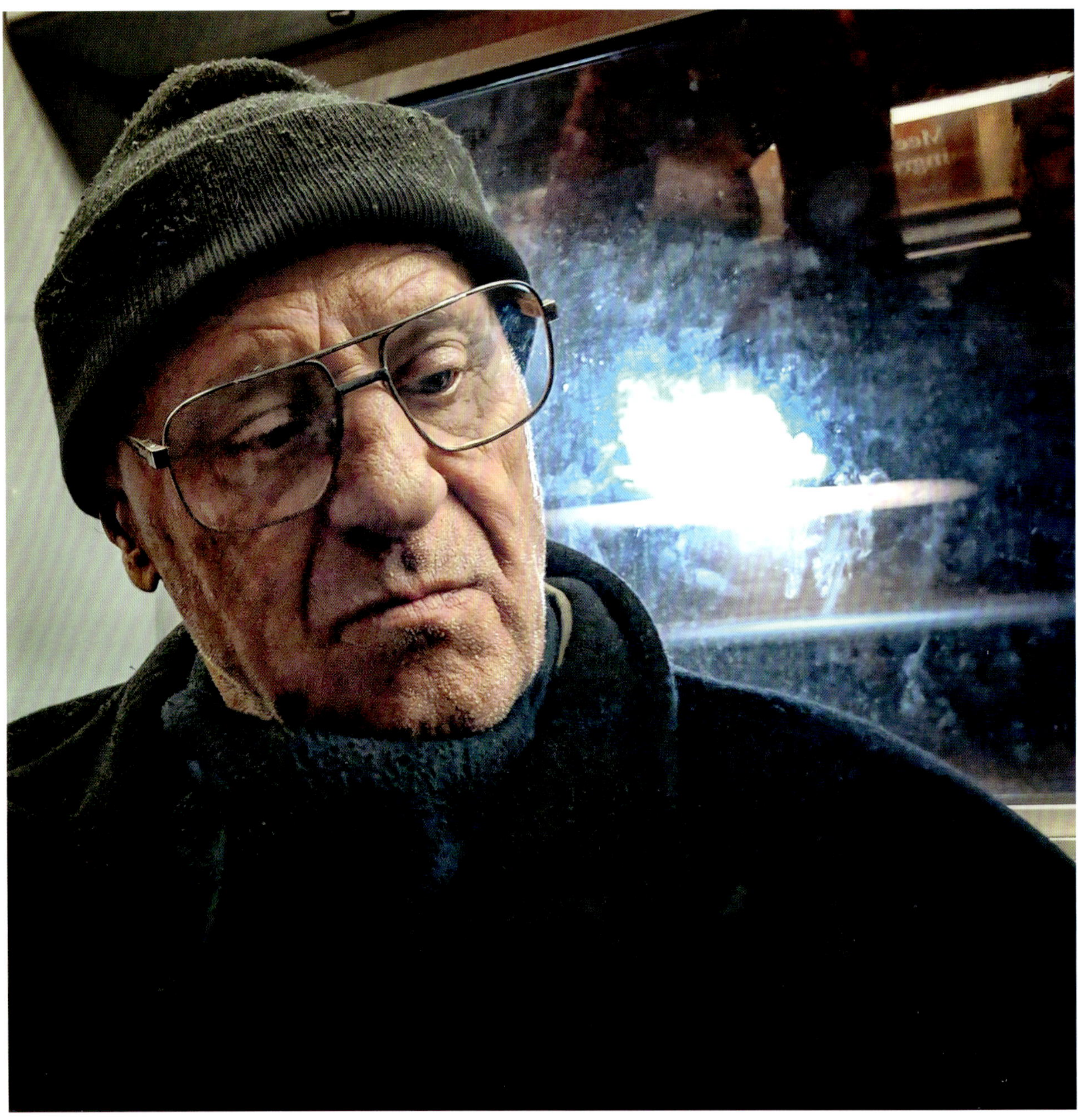

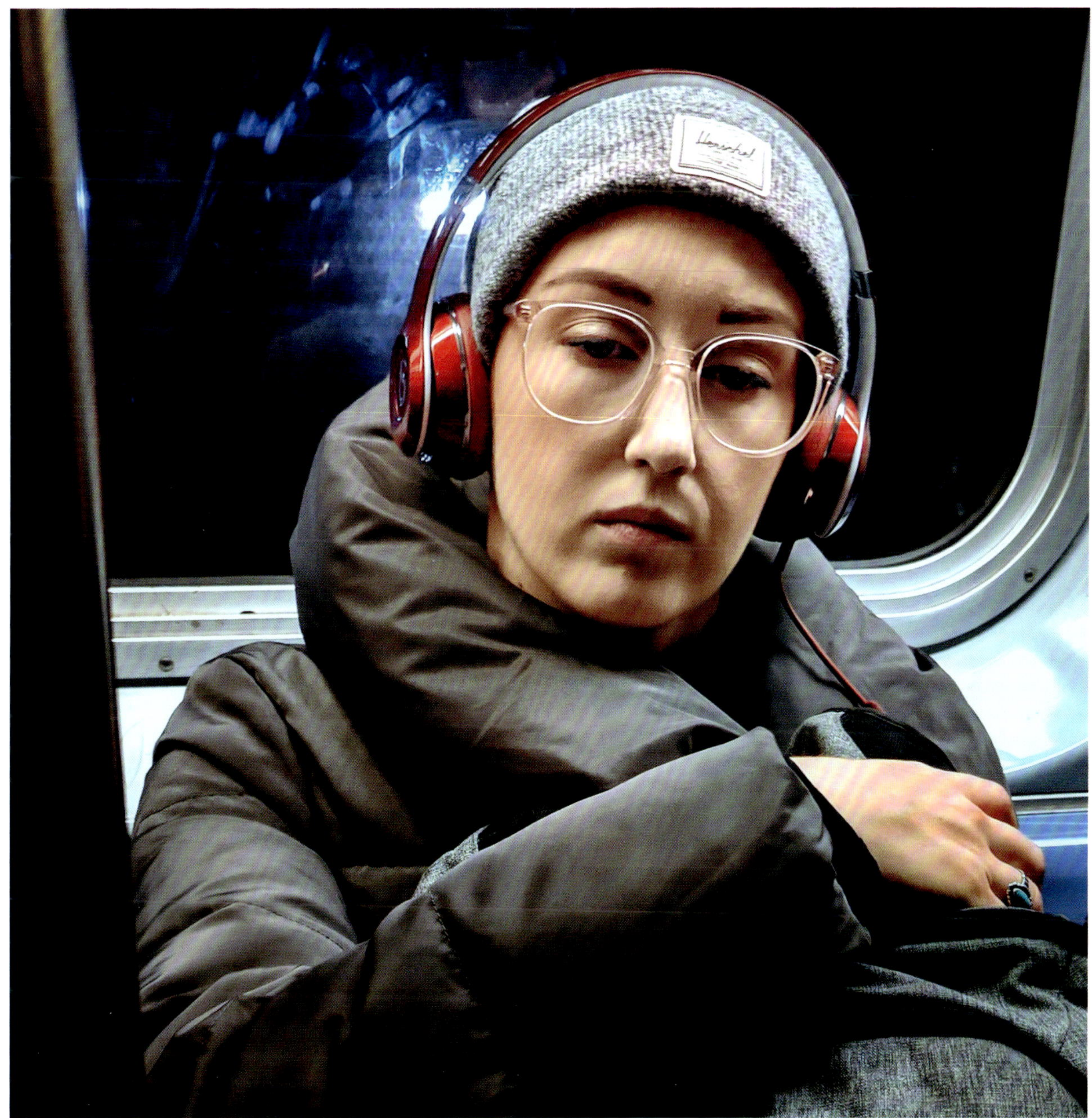

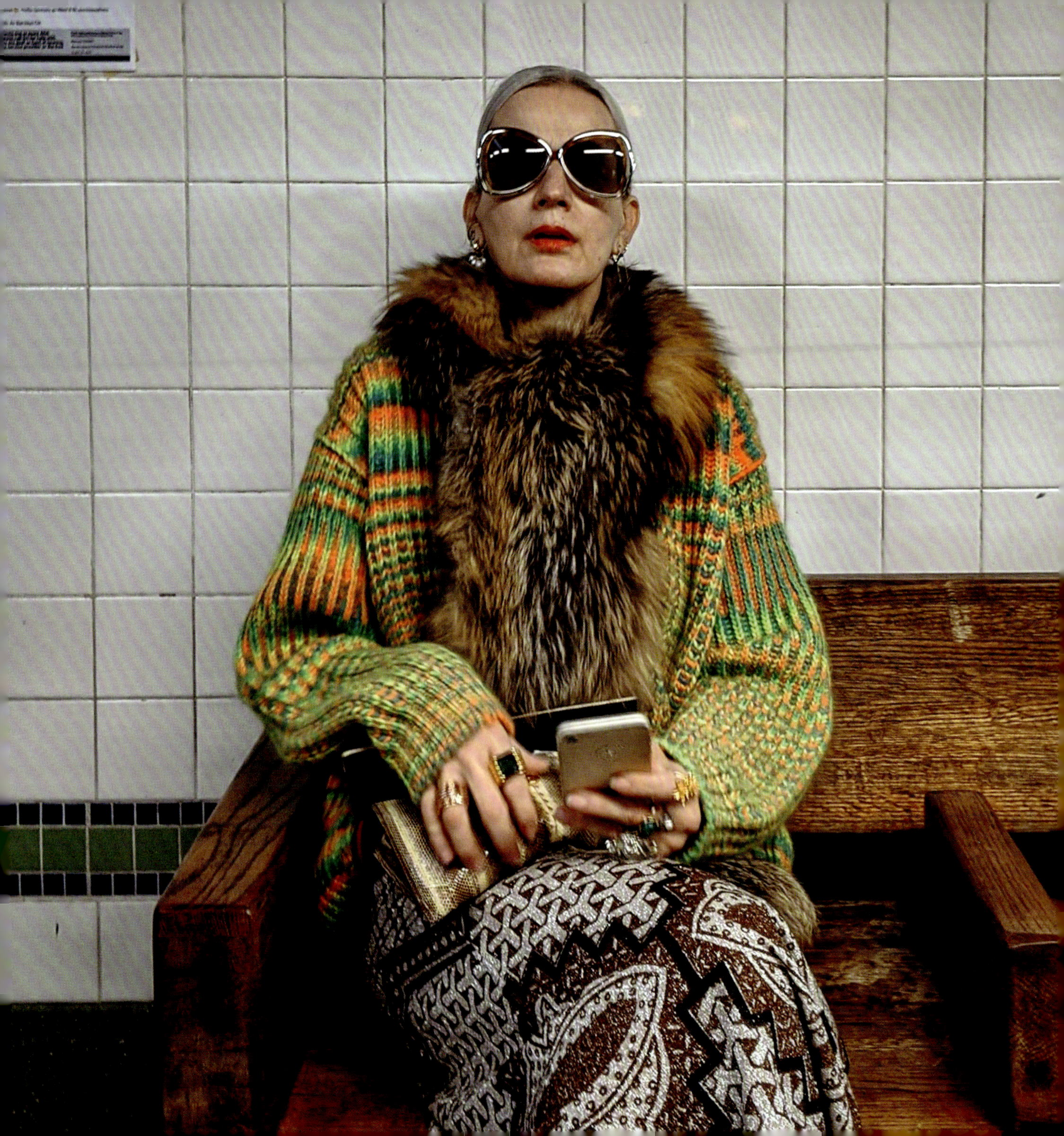

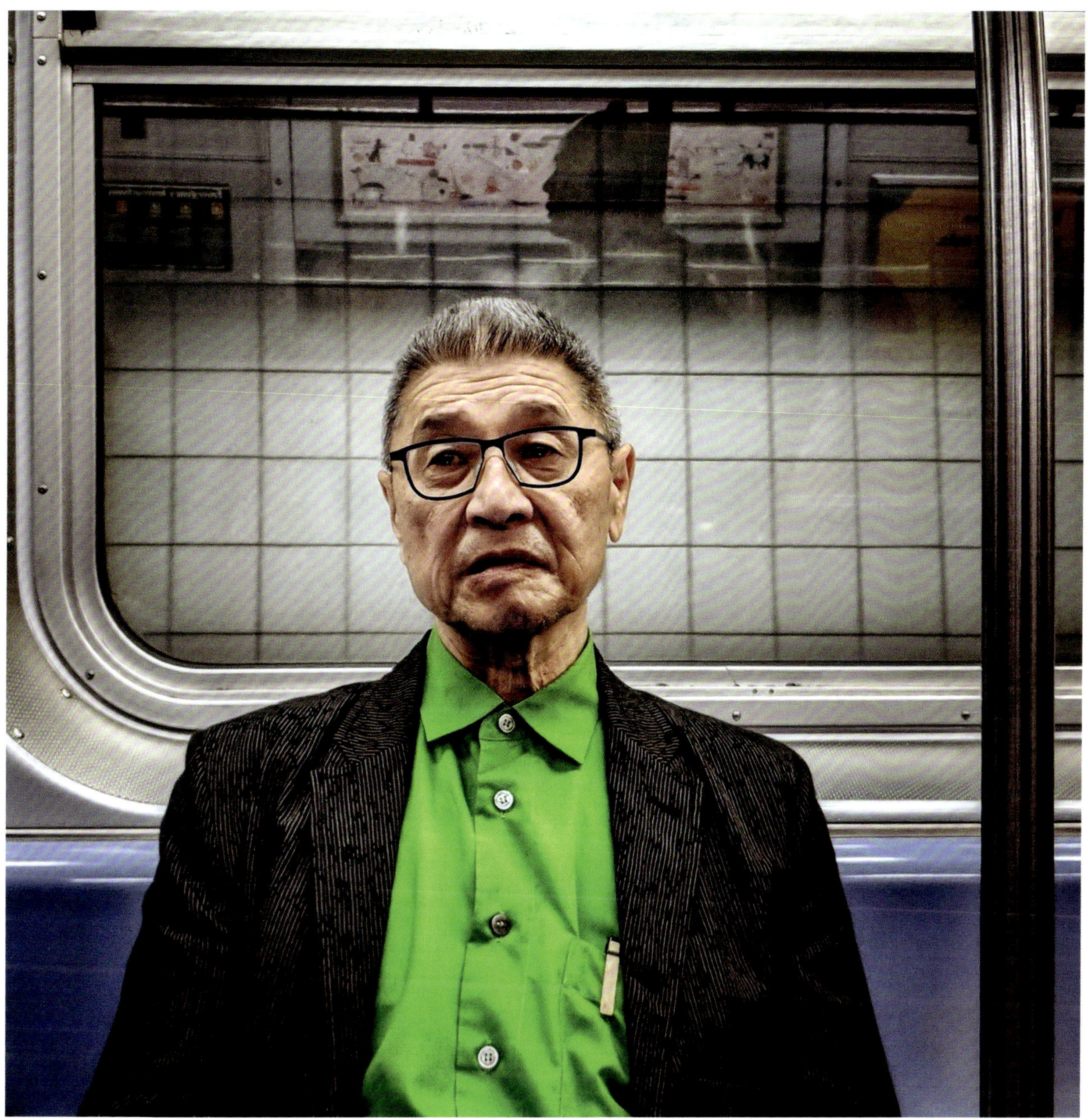

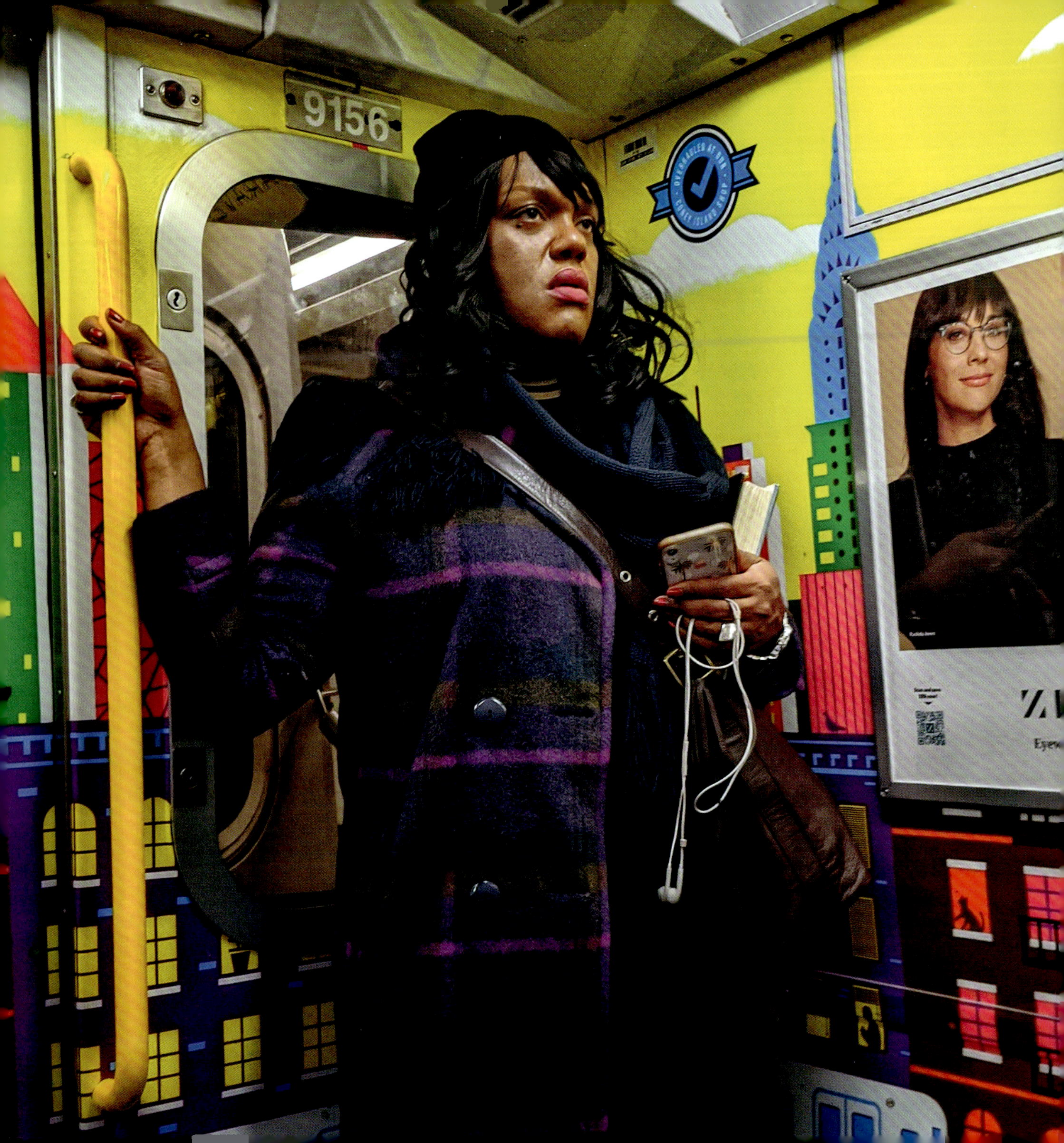

9156

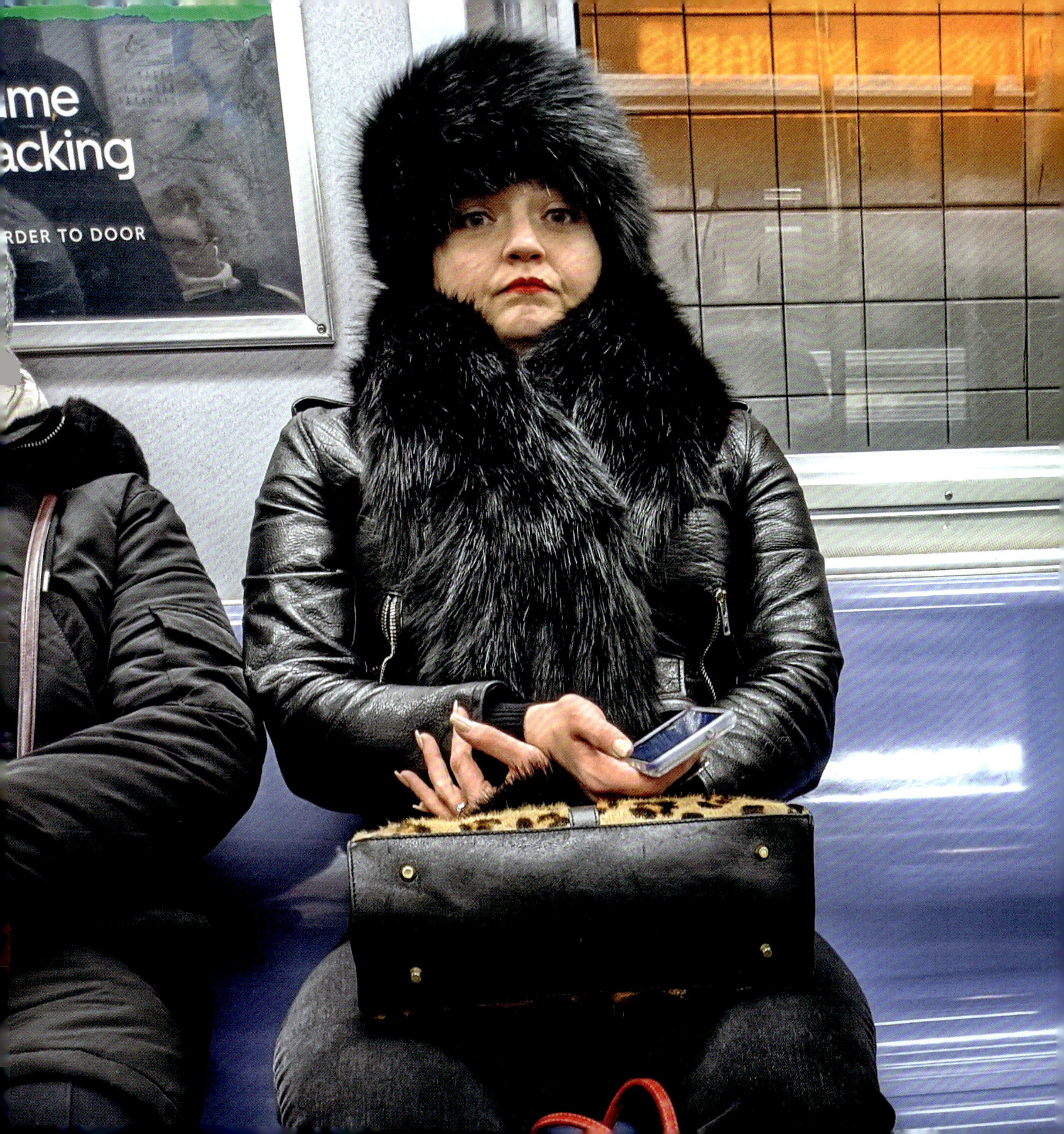
me
acking
RDER TO DOOR

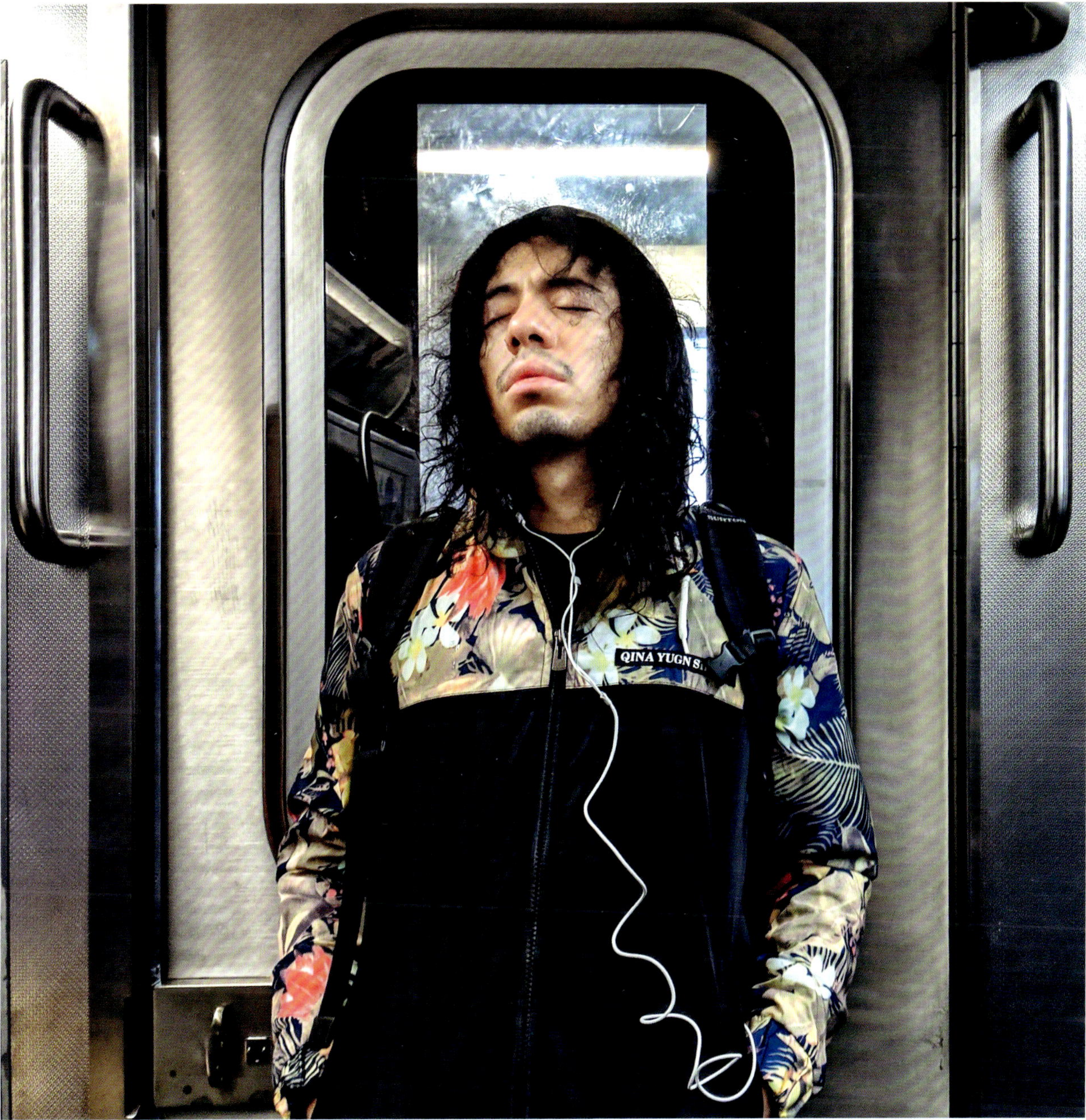
QINA YUGN S

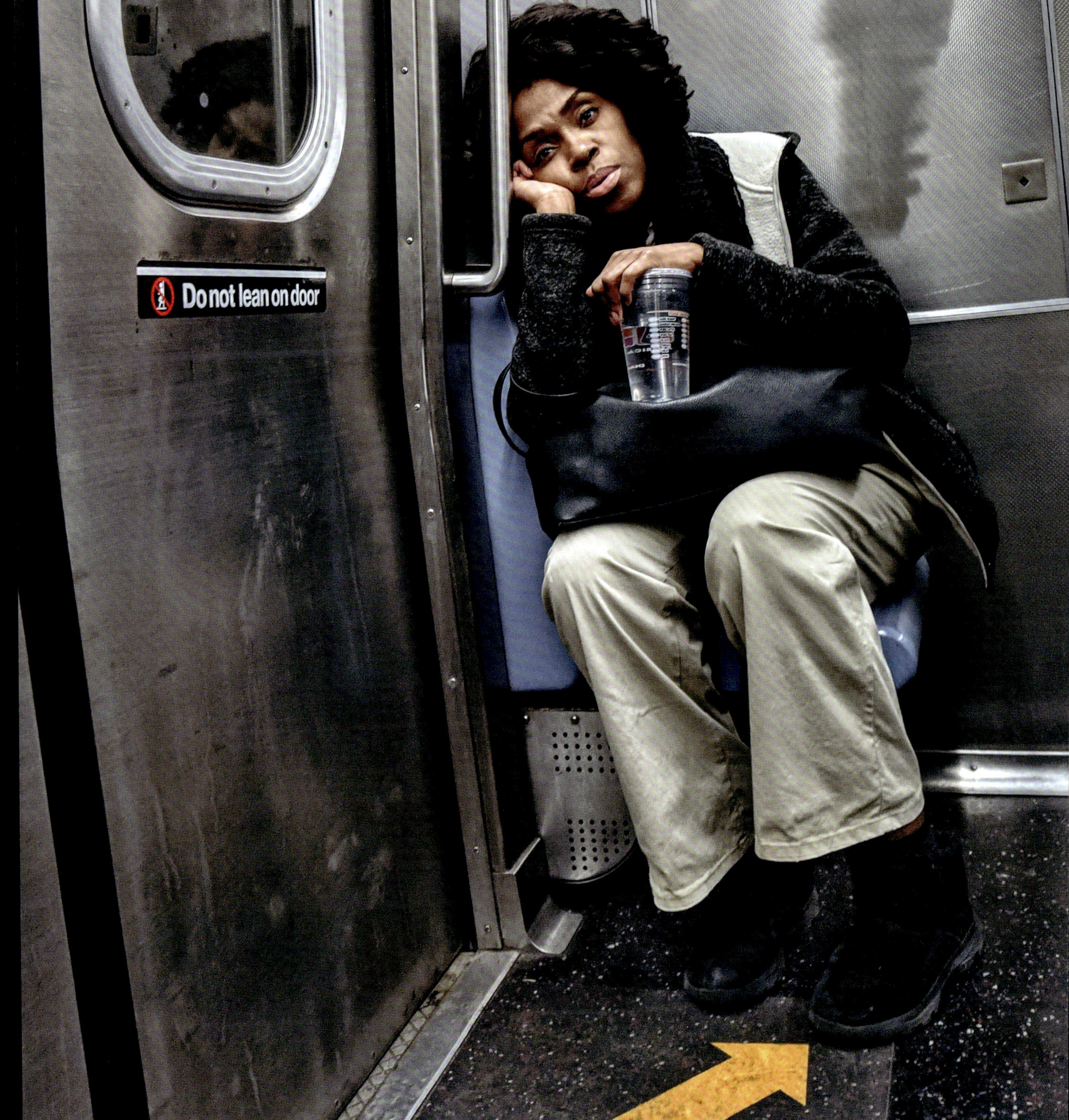
Do not lean on door

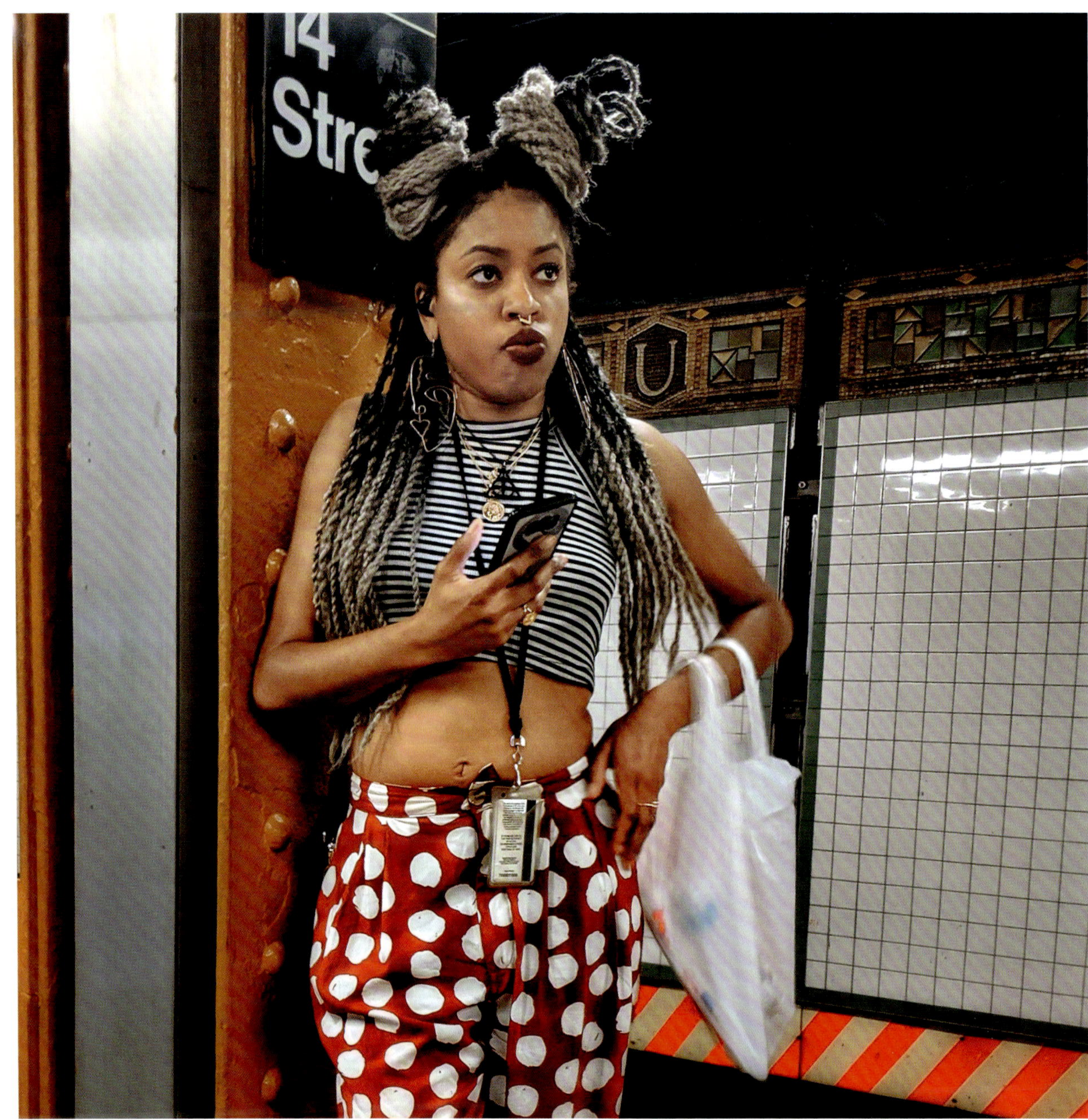
14
Str

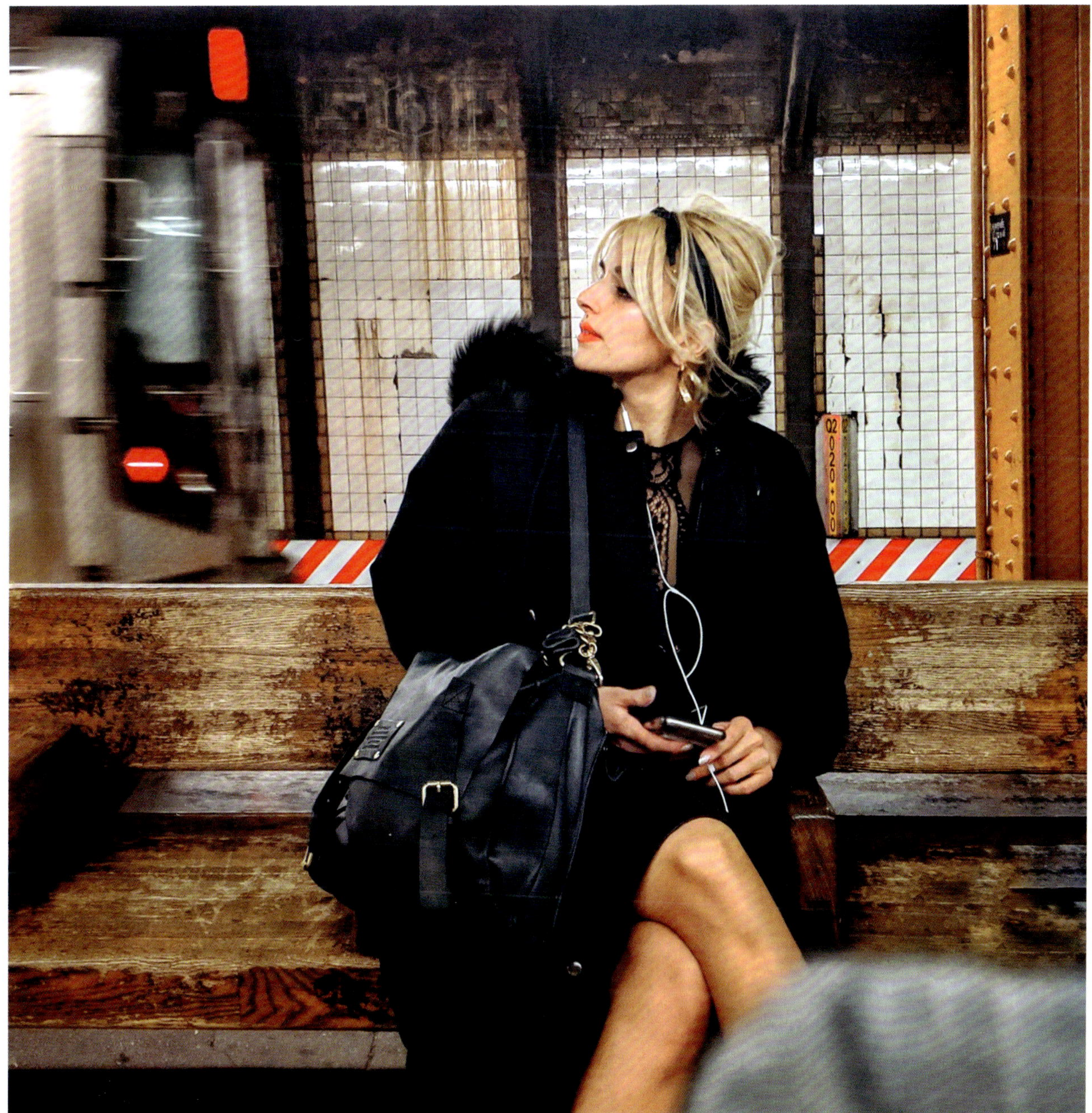

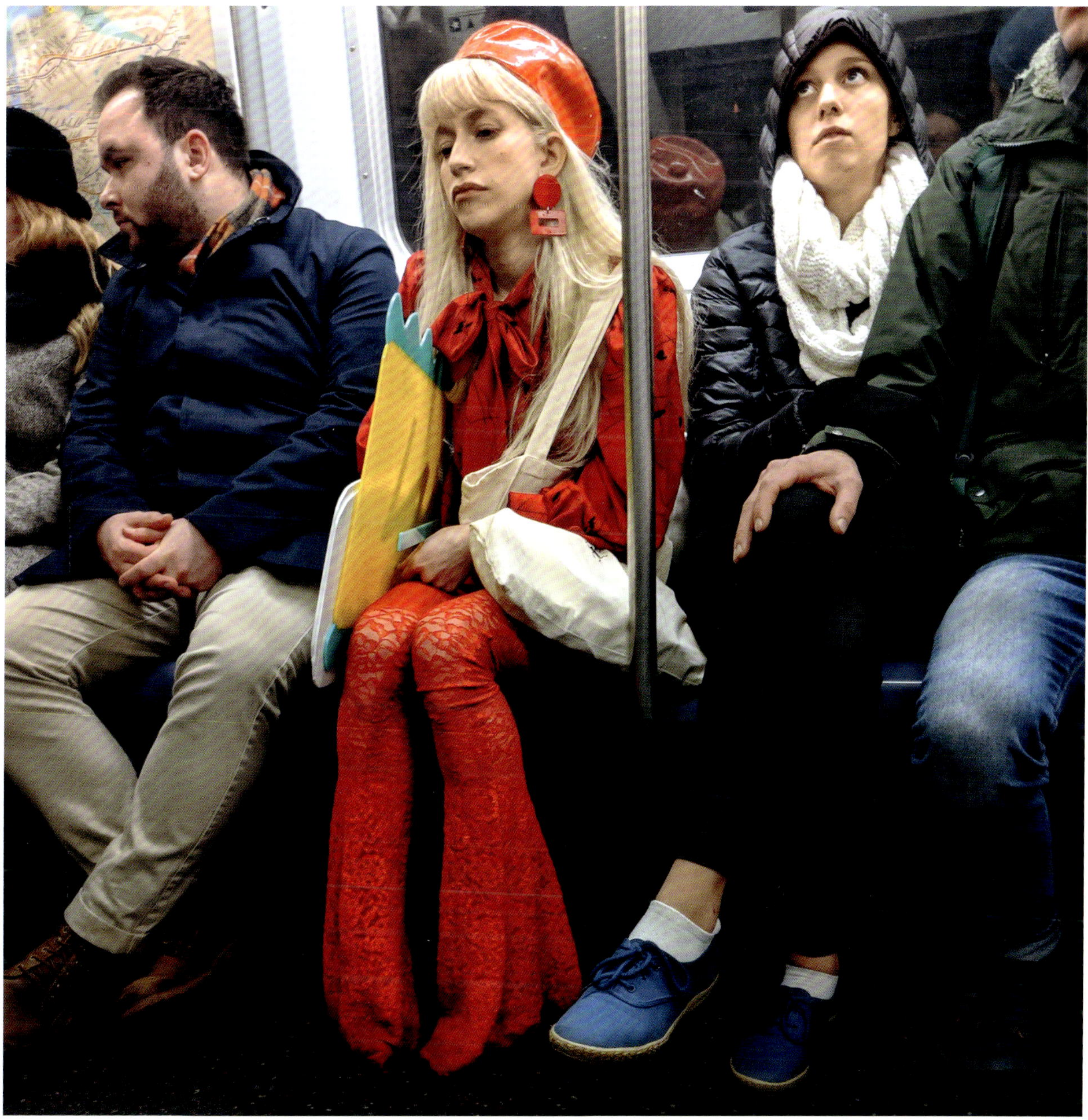

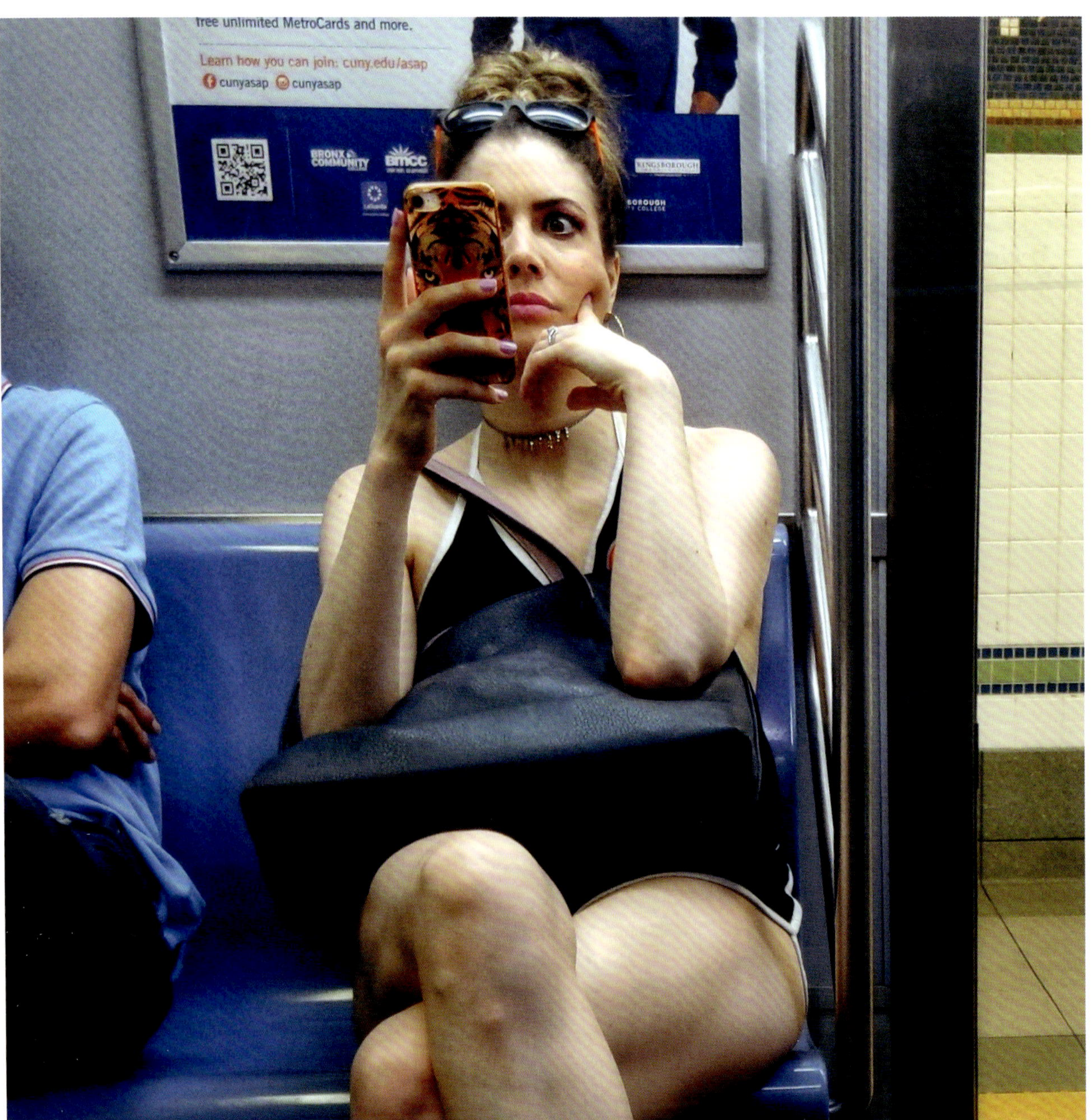
free unlimited MetroCards and more.
Learn how you can join: cuny.edu/asap
cunyasap   cunyasap
BRONX COMMUNITY
BMCC
KINGSBOROUGH
BOROUGH CITY COLLEGE

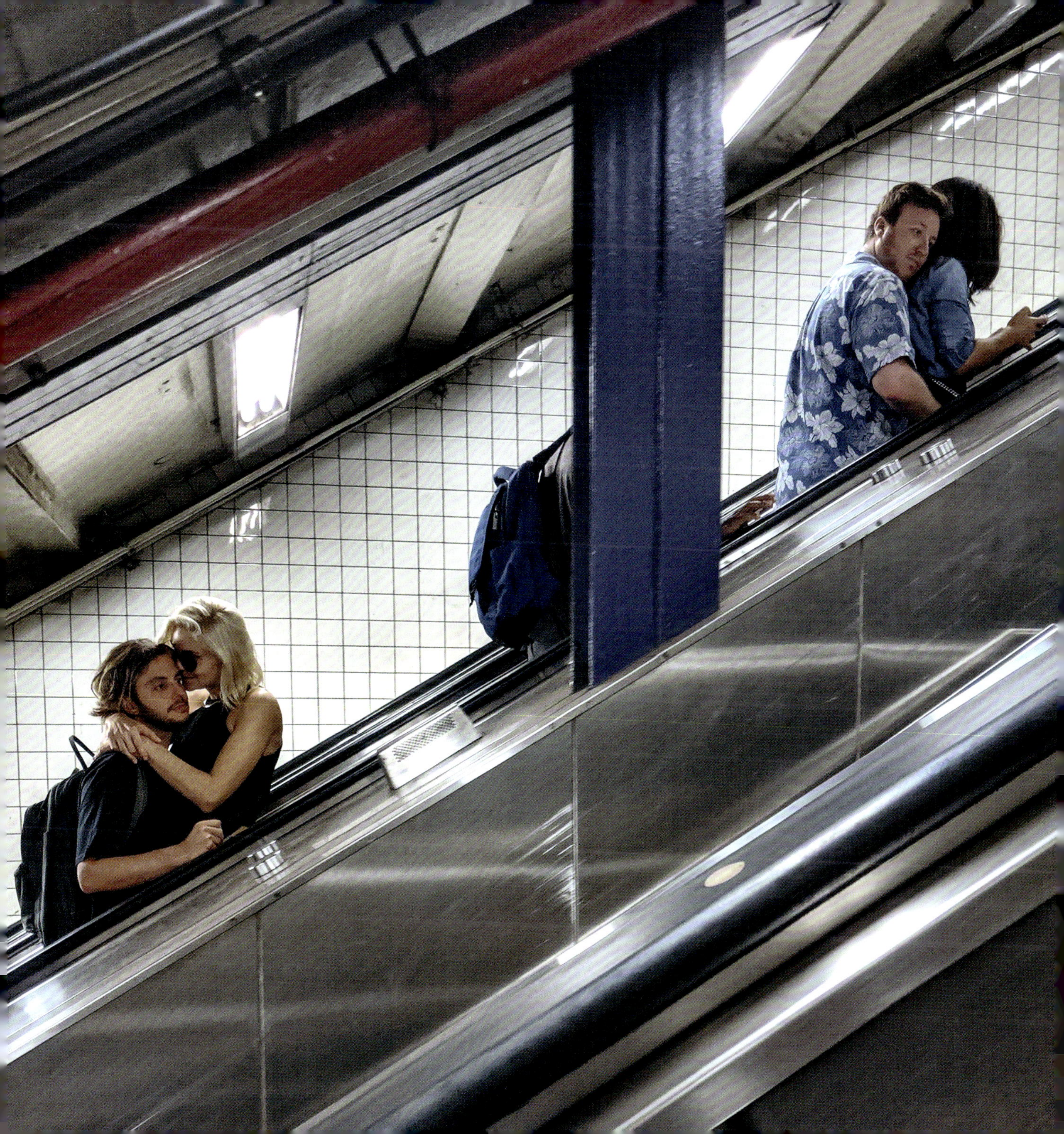

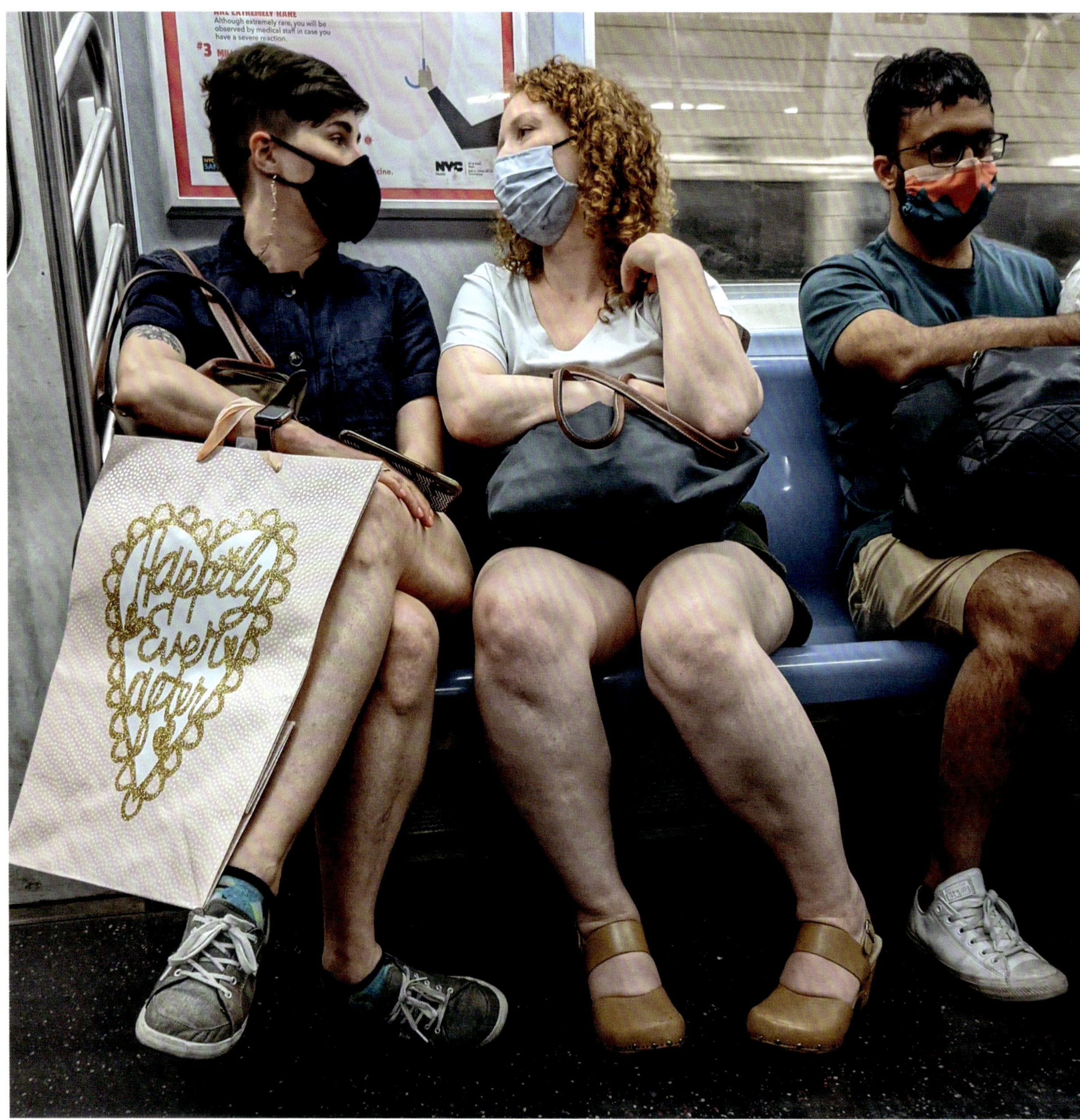

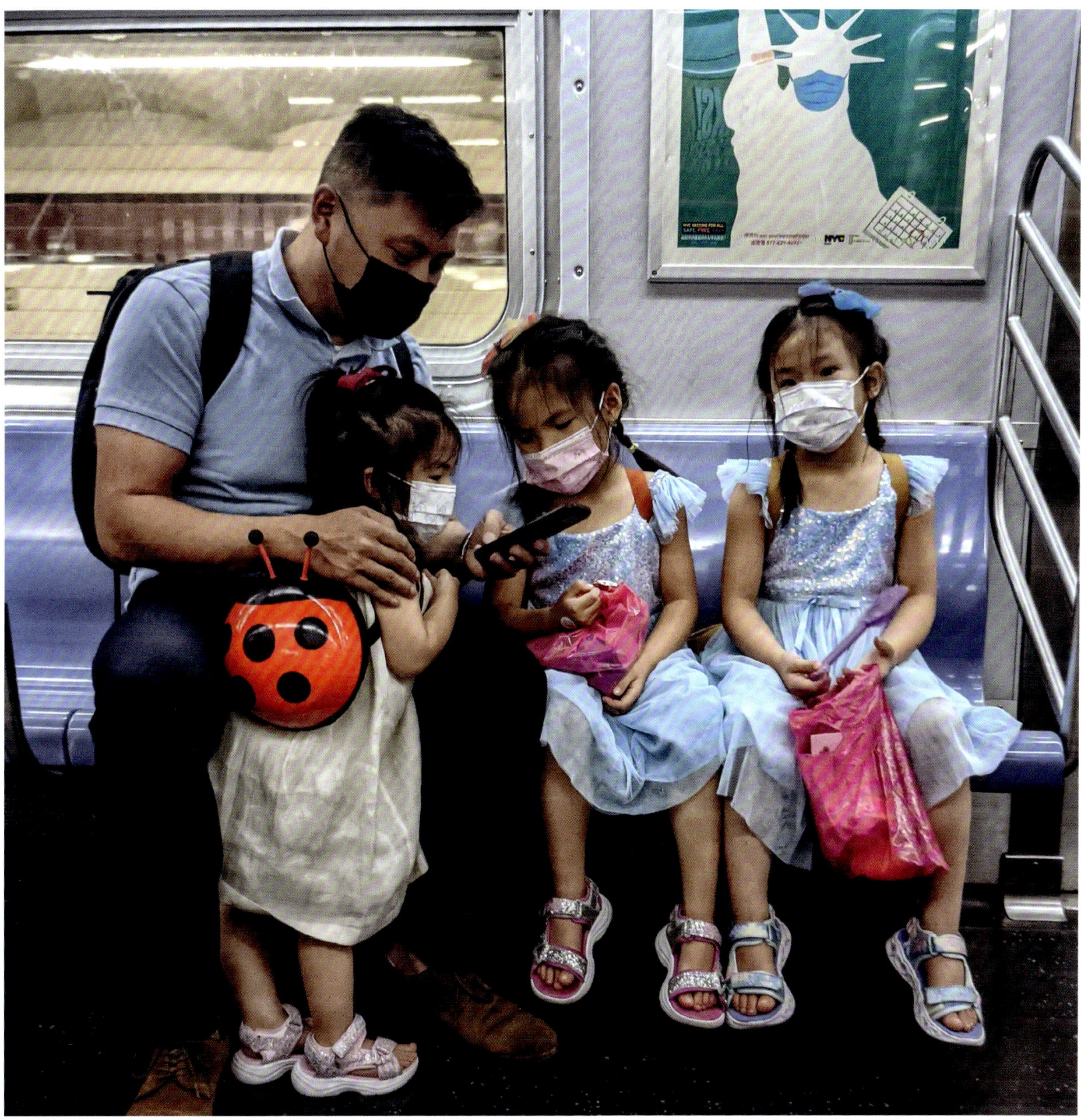

NYC VACCINE FOR ALL.
SAFE. FREE.
877-829-4692
NYC

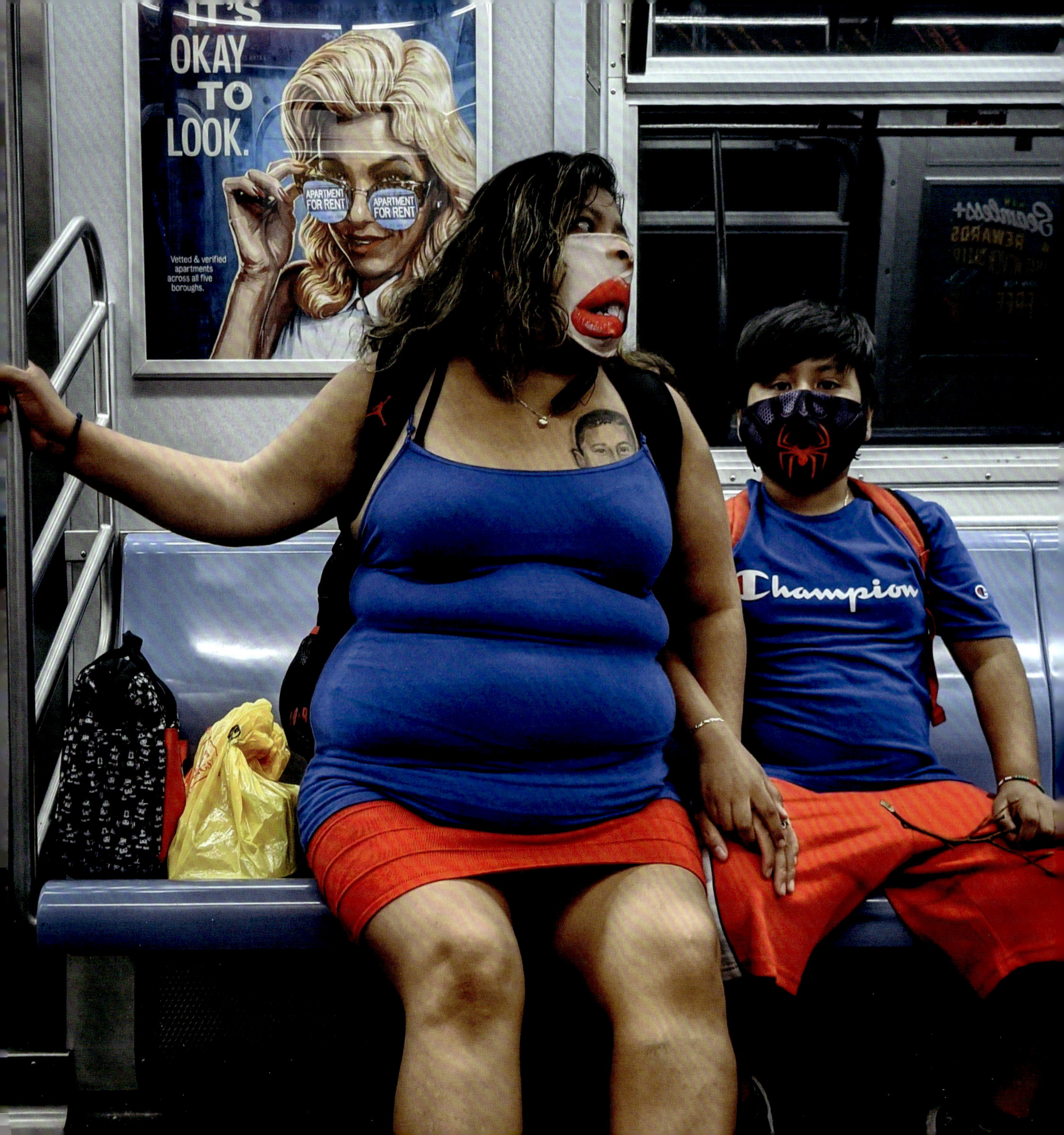
IT'S
OKAY
TO
LOOK.
APARTMENT
FOR RENT
APARTMENT
FOR RENT
Vetted & verified
apartments
across all five
boroughs.
Champion

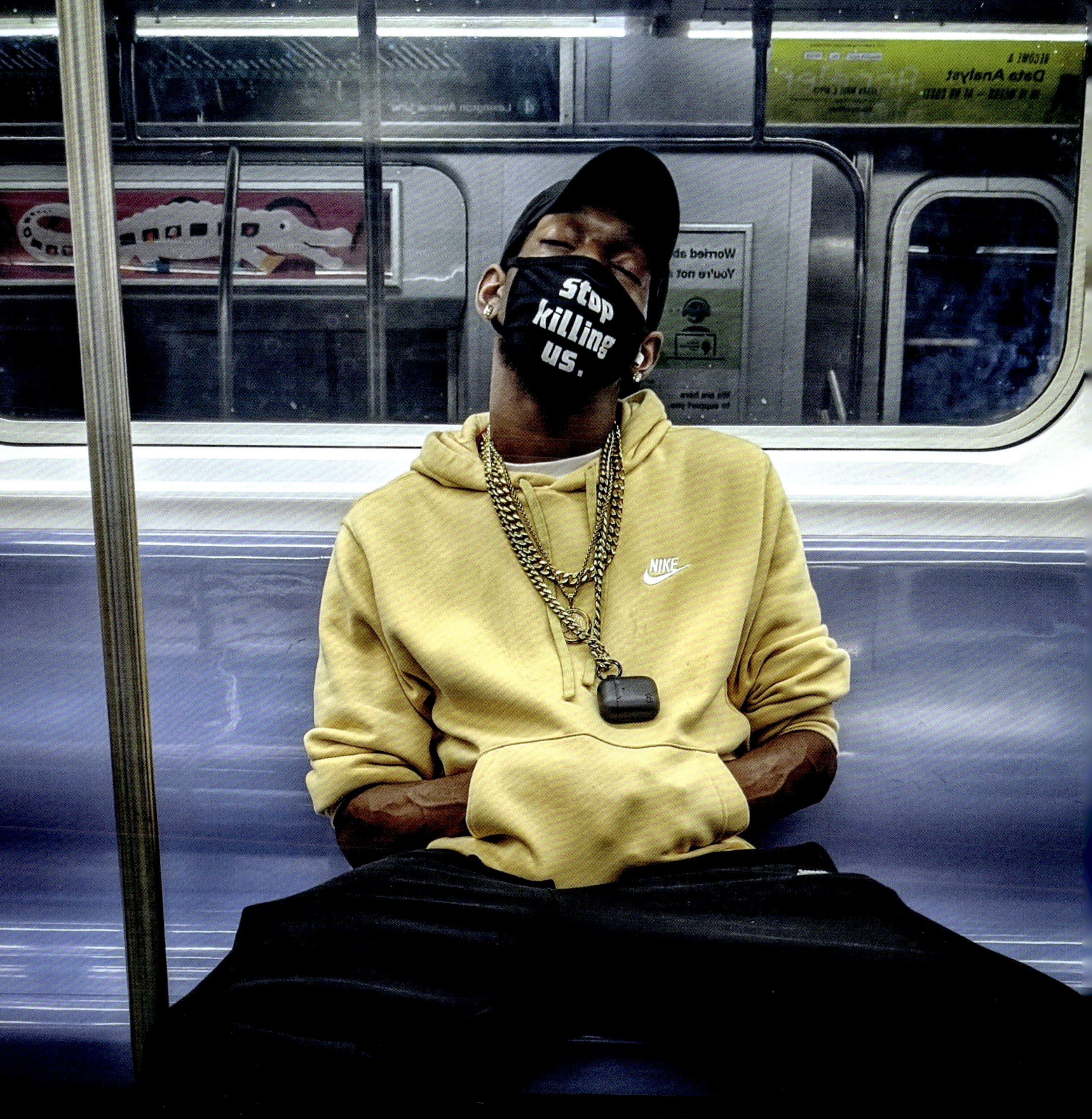

stop
killing
us.
NIKE

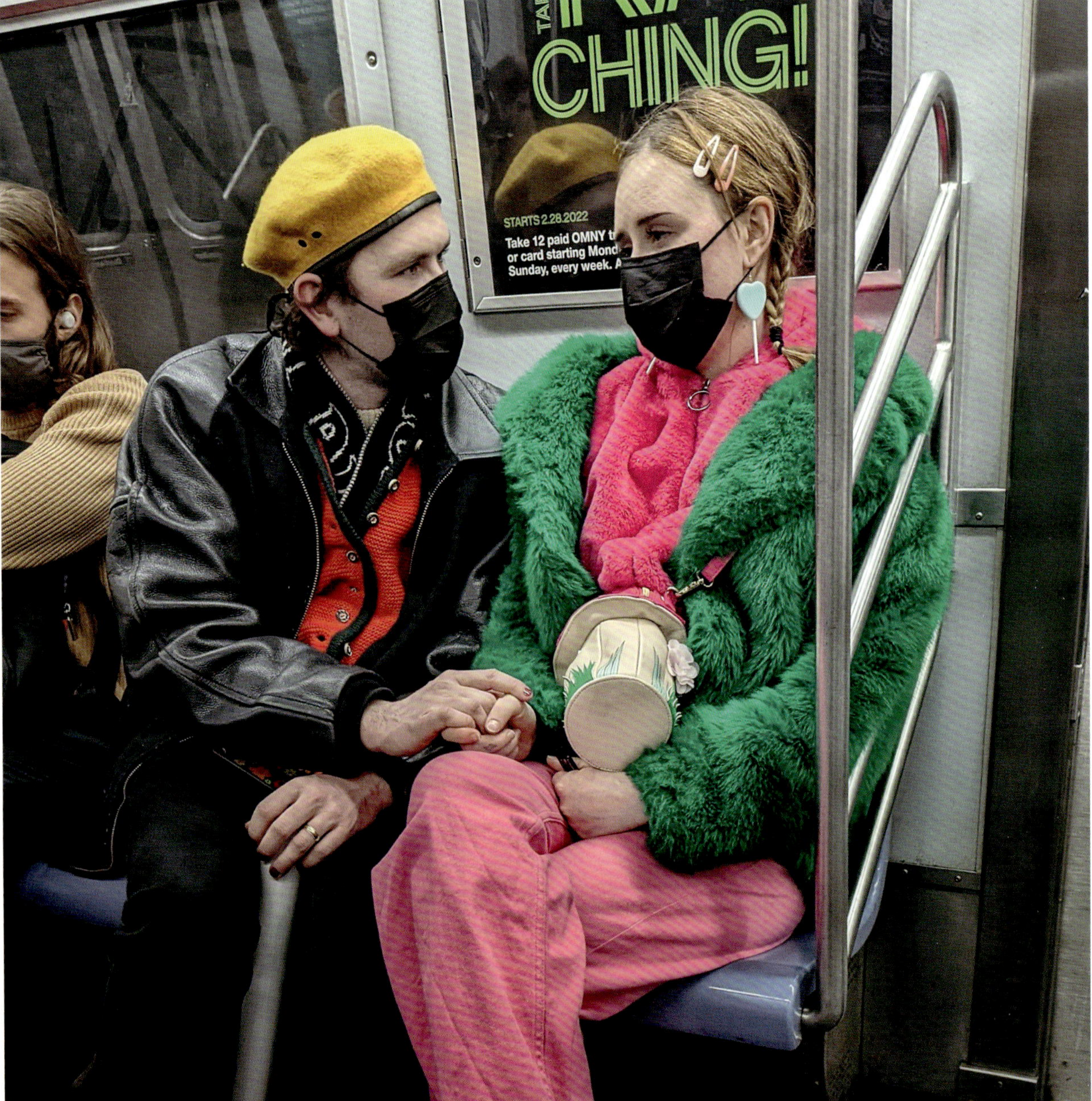
CHING!
STARTS 2.28.2022
Take 12 paid OMNY tr
or card starting Mond
Sunday, every week. A

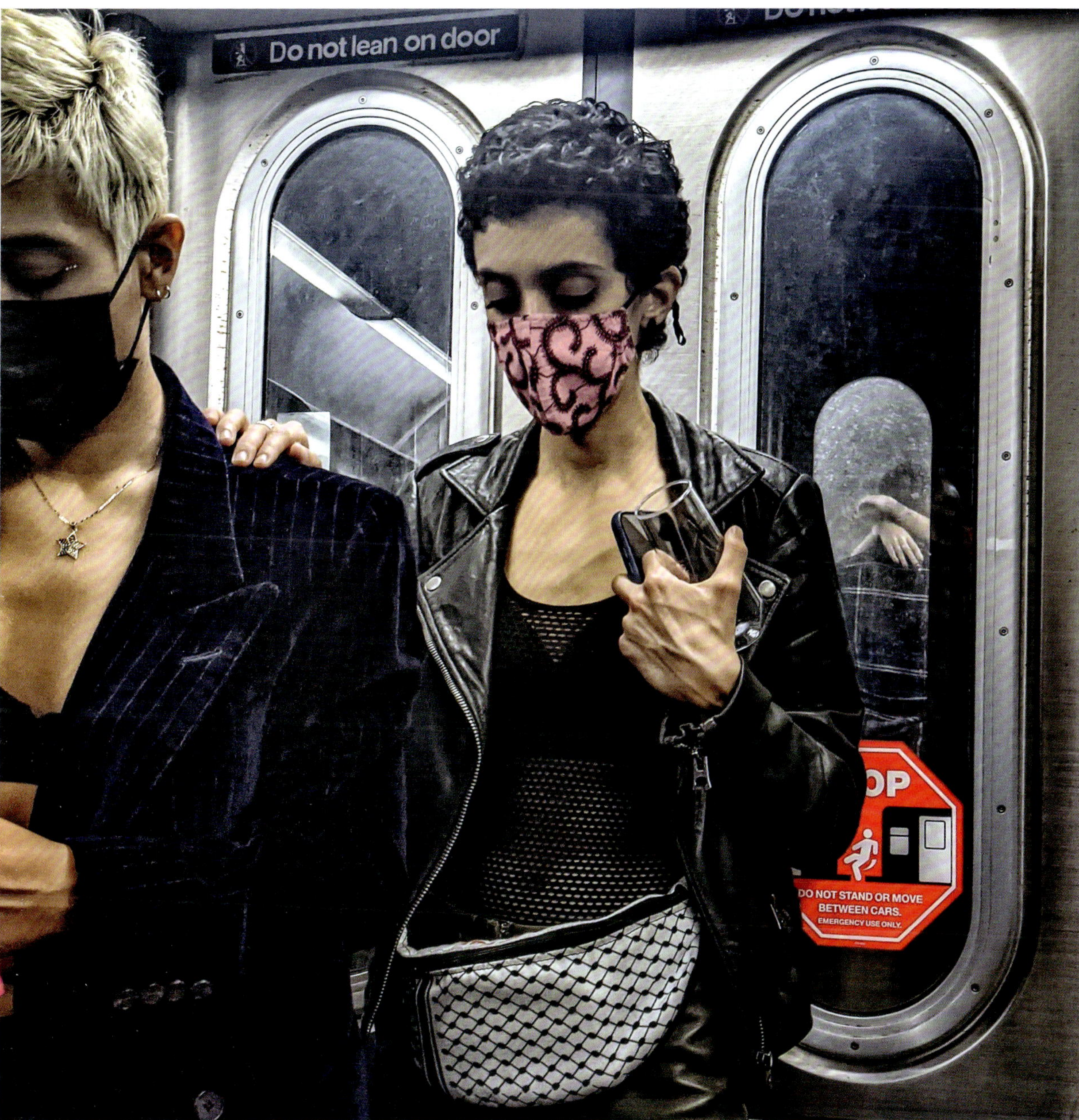
Do not lean on door
STOP
DO NOT STAND OR MOVE
BETWEEN CARS.
EMERGENCY USE ONLY.

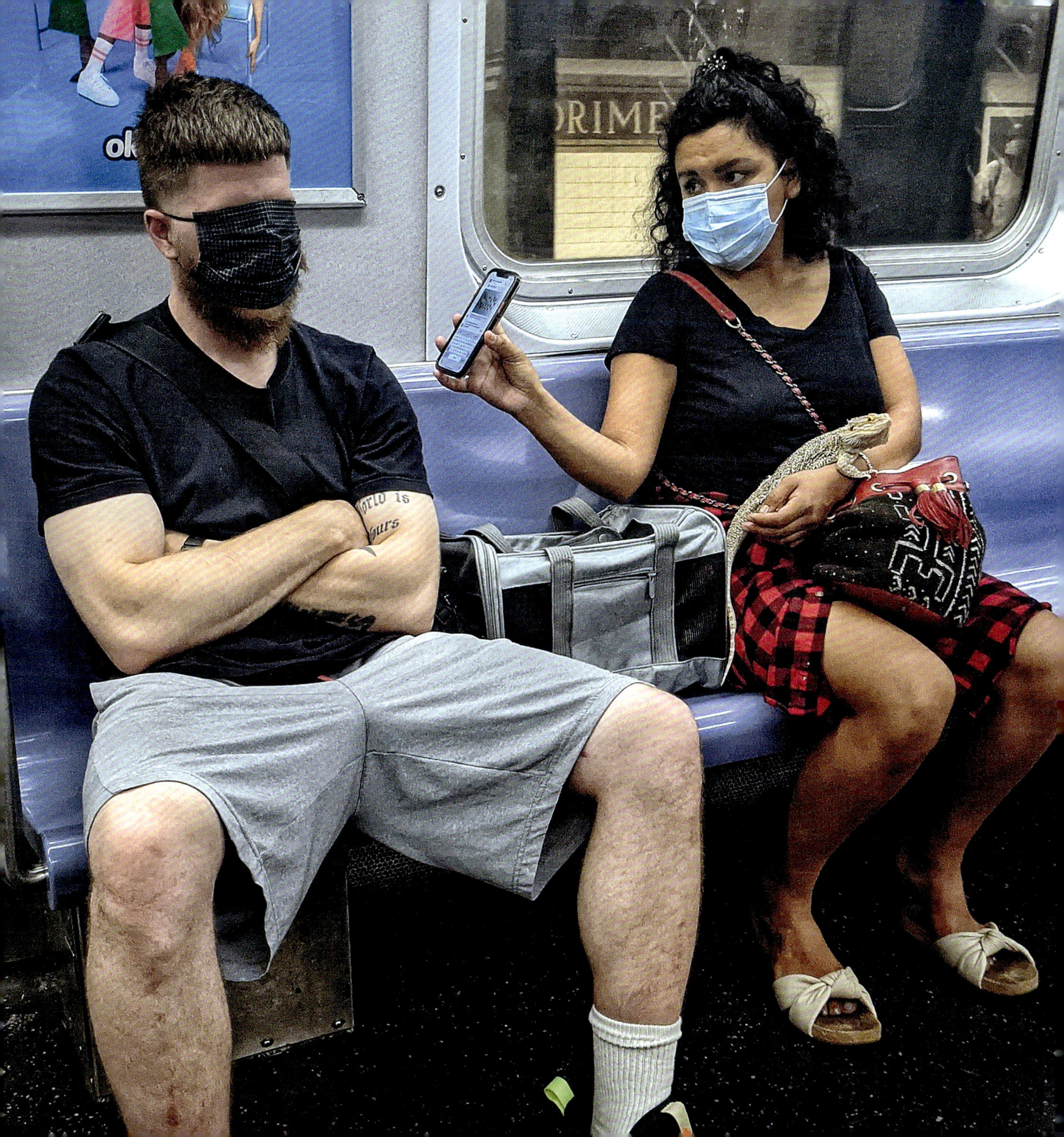

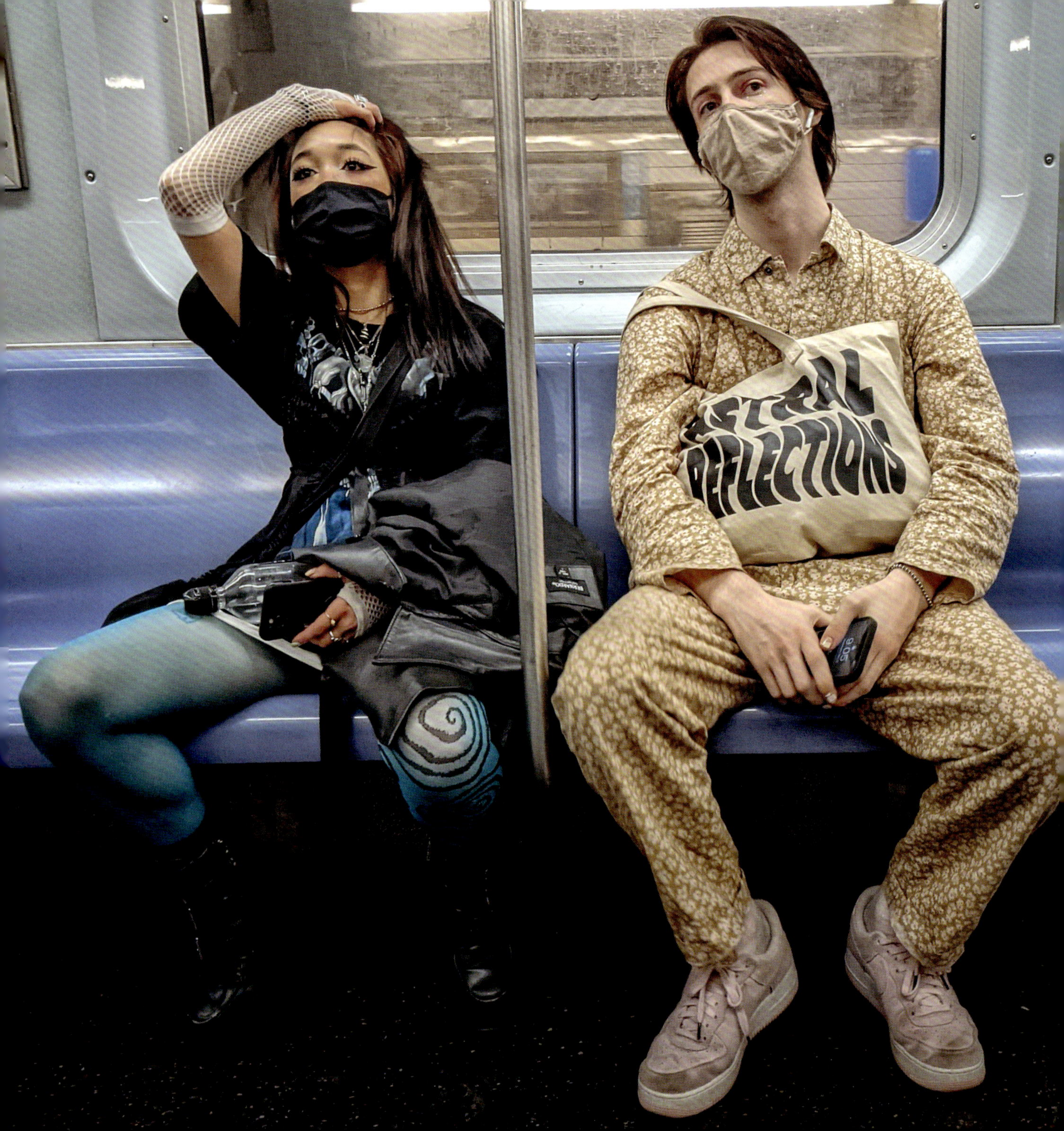
ASTRAL
REFLECTIONS

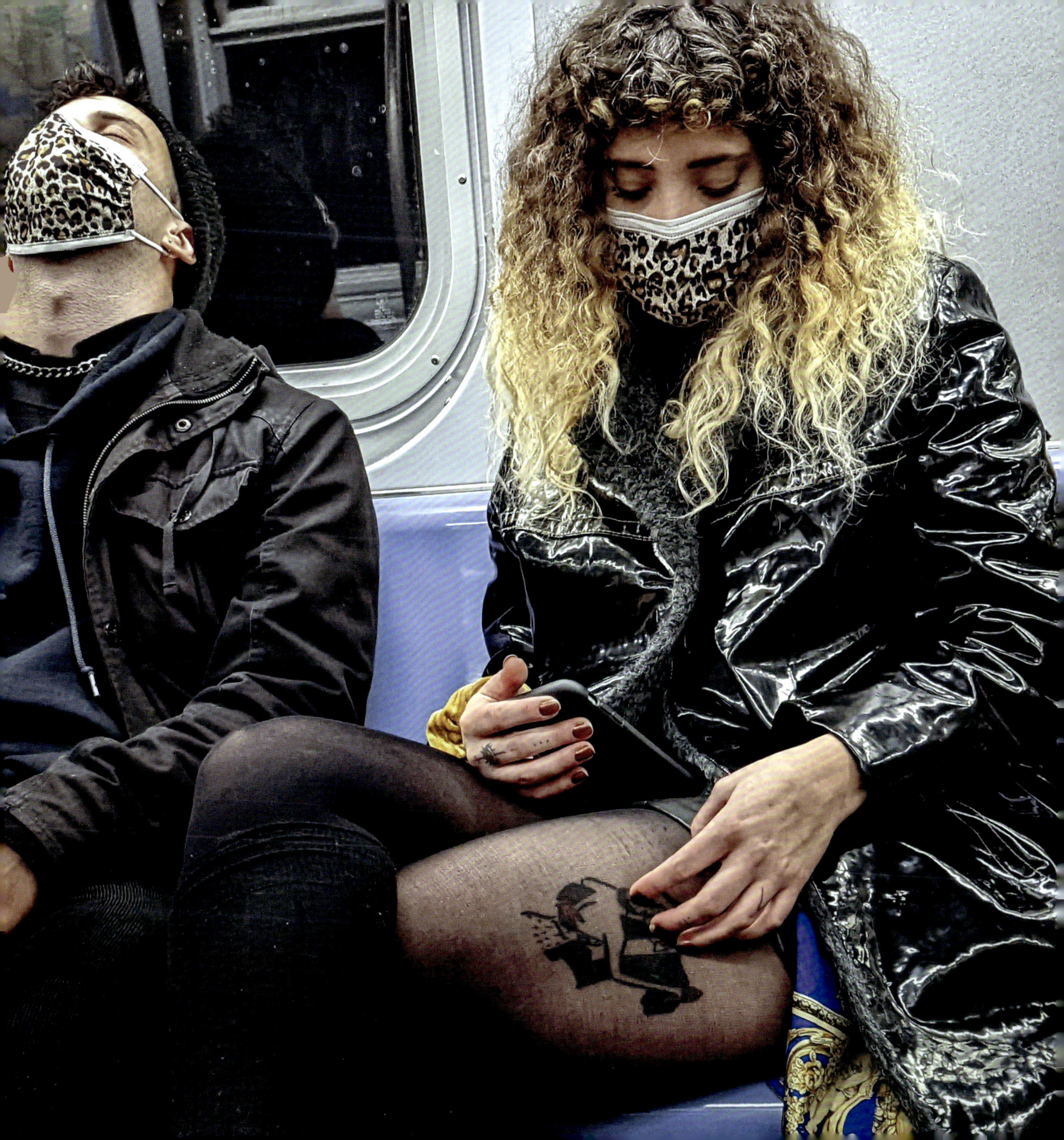

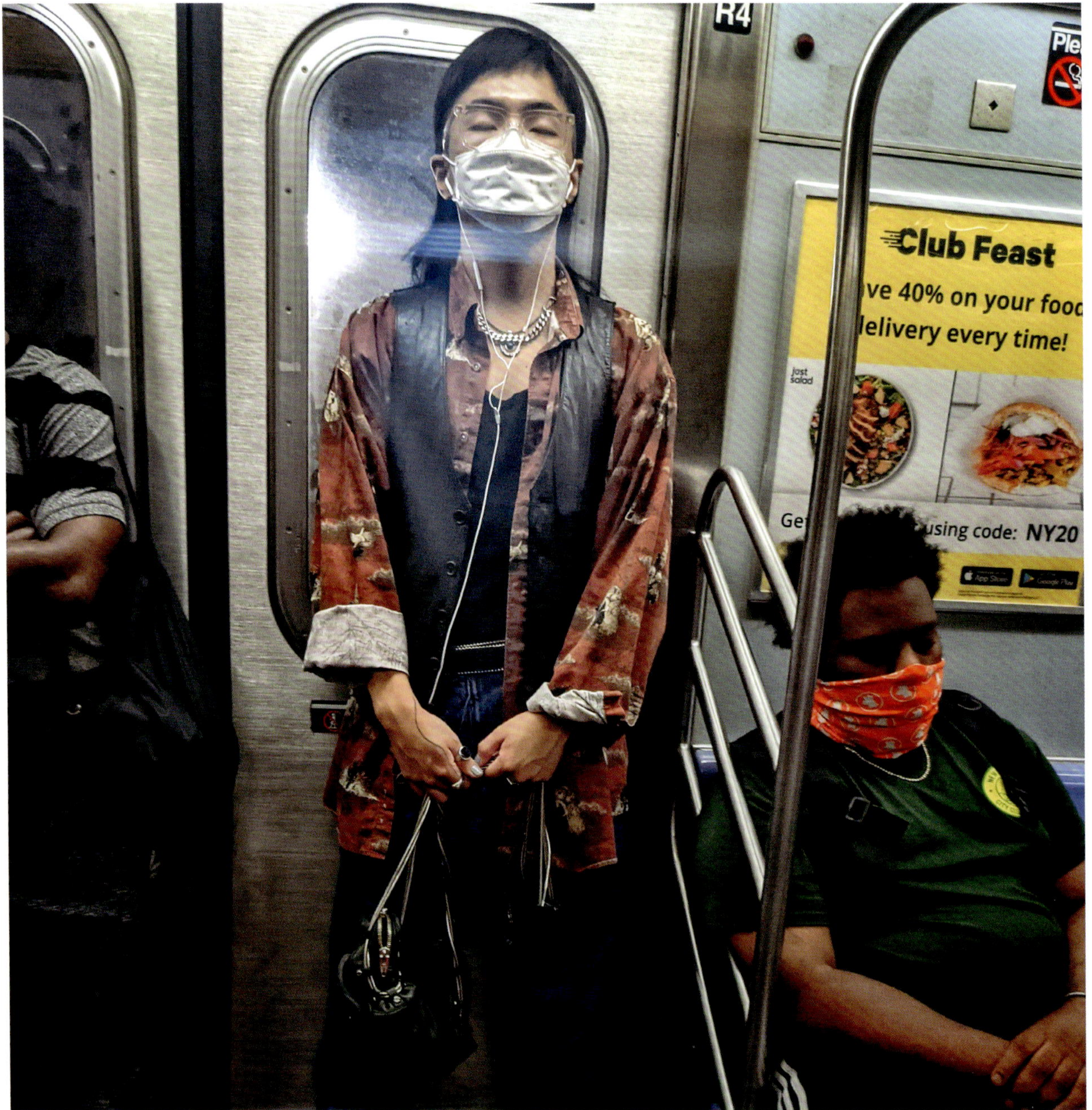
R4
Club Feast
ve 40% on your food
elivery every time!
just salad
Get   using code: NY20
App Store   Google Play
Ple

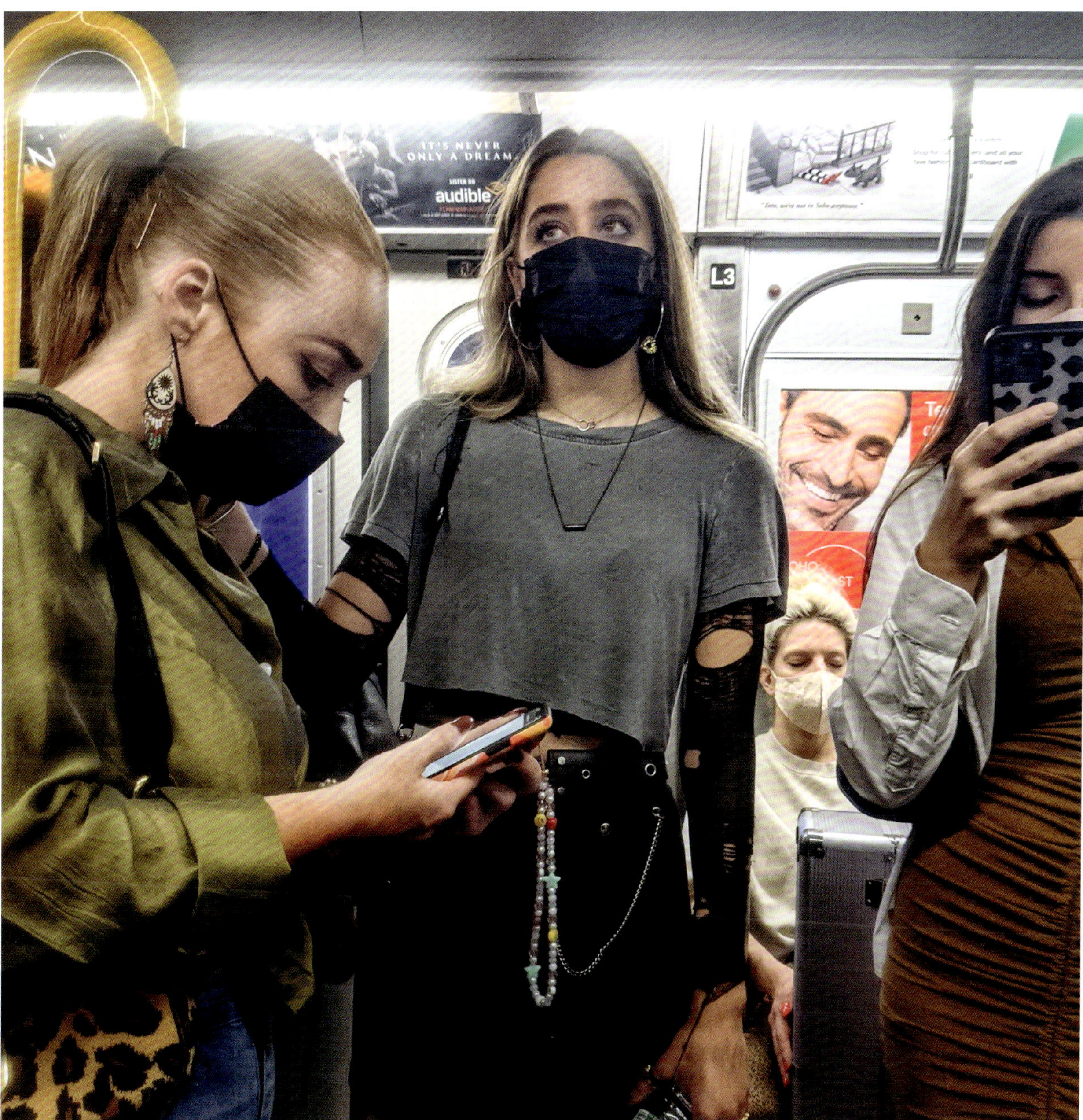

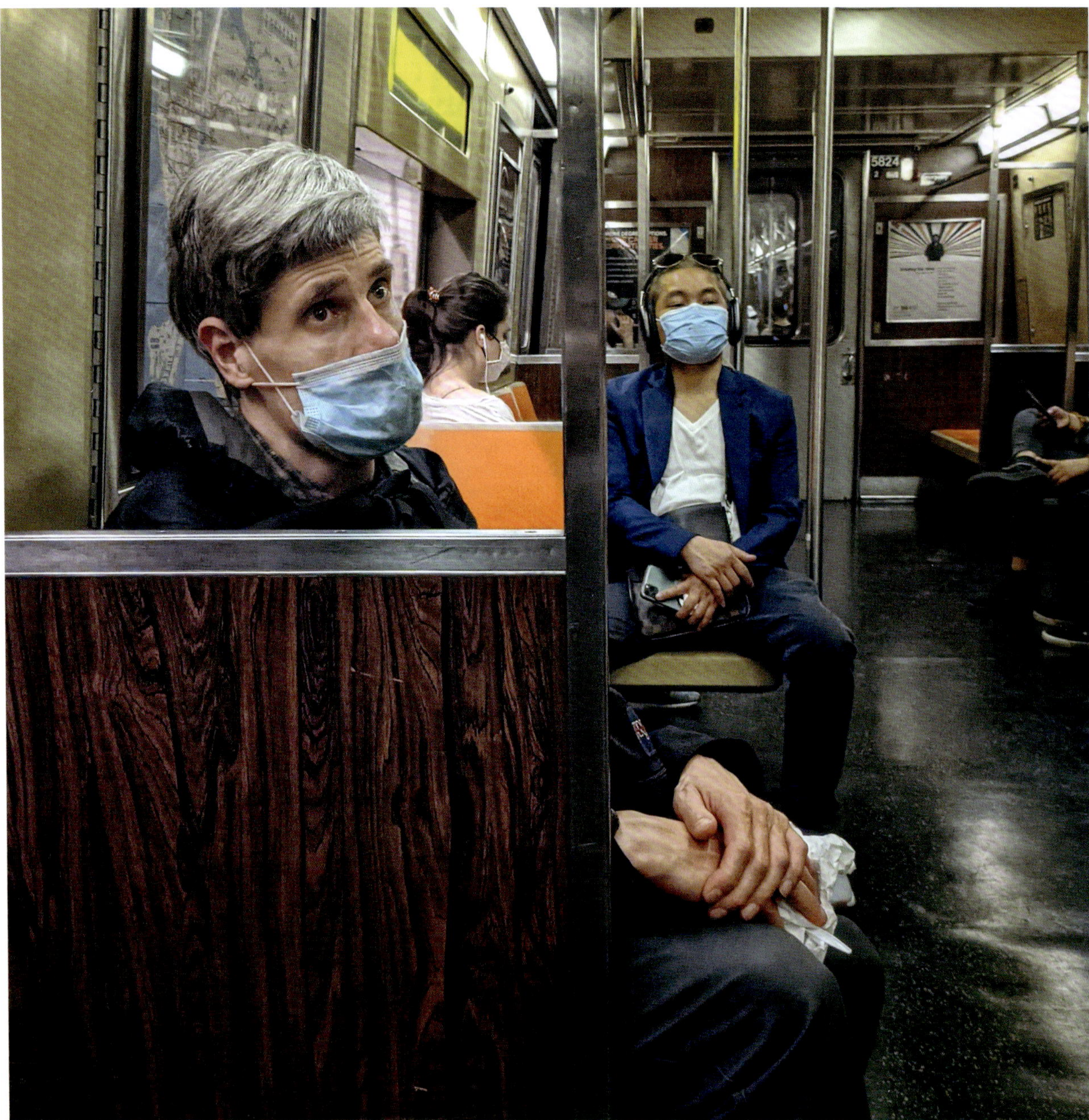

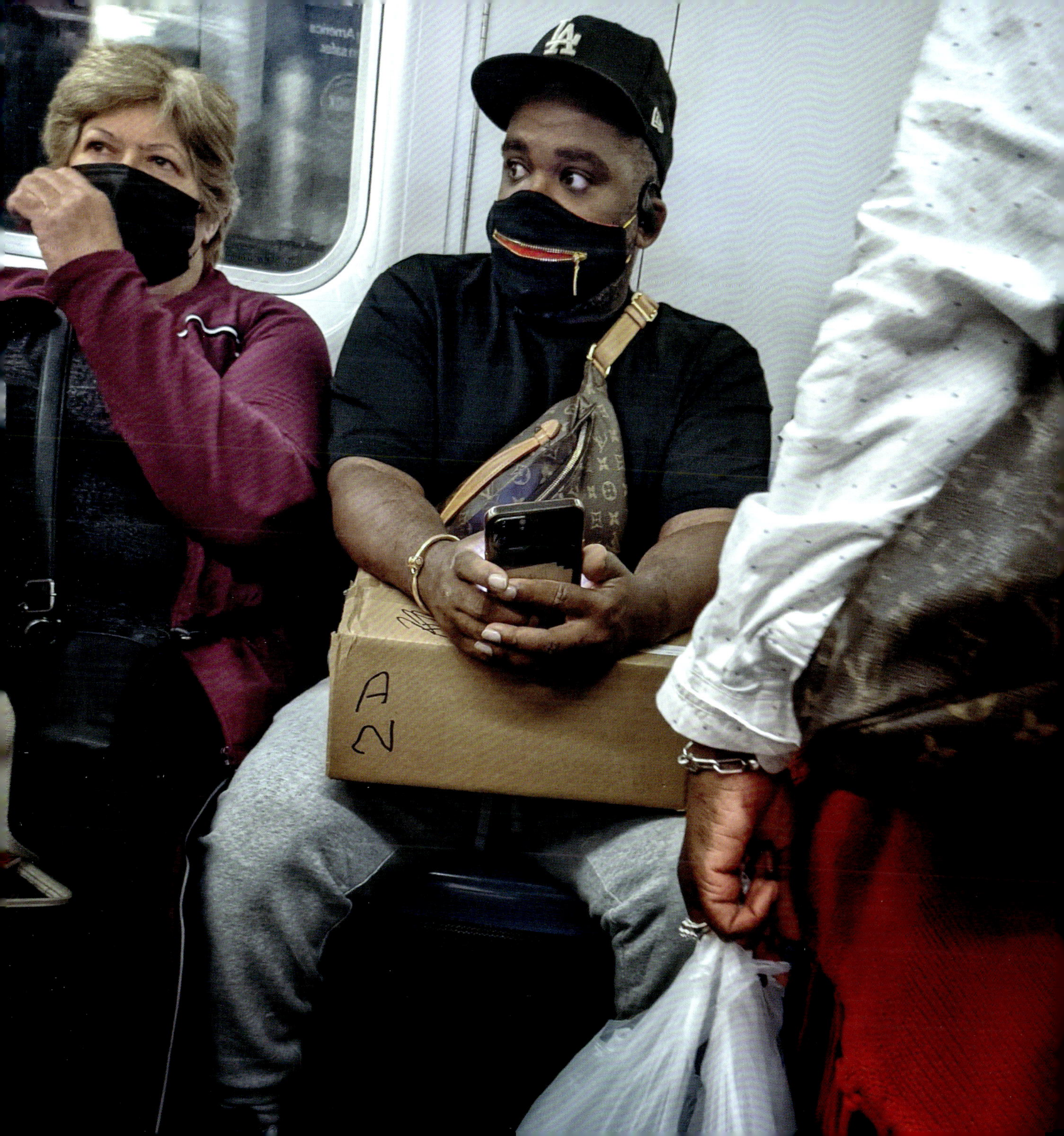

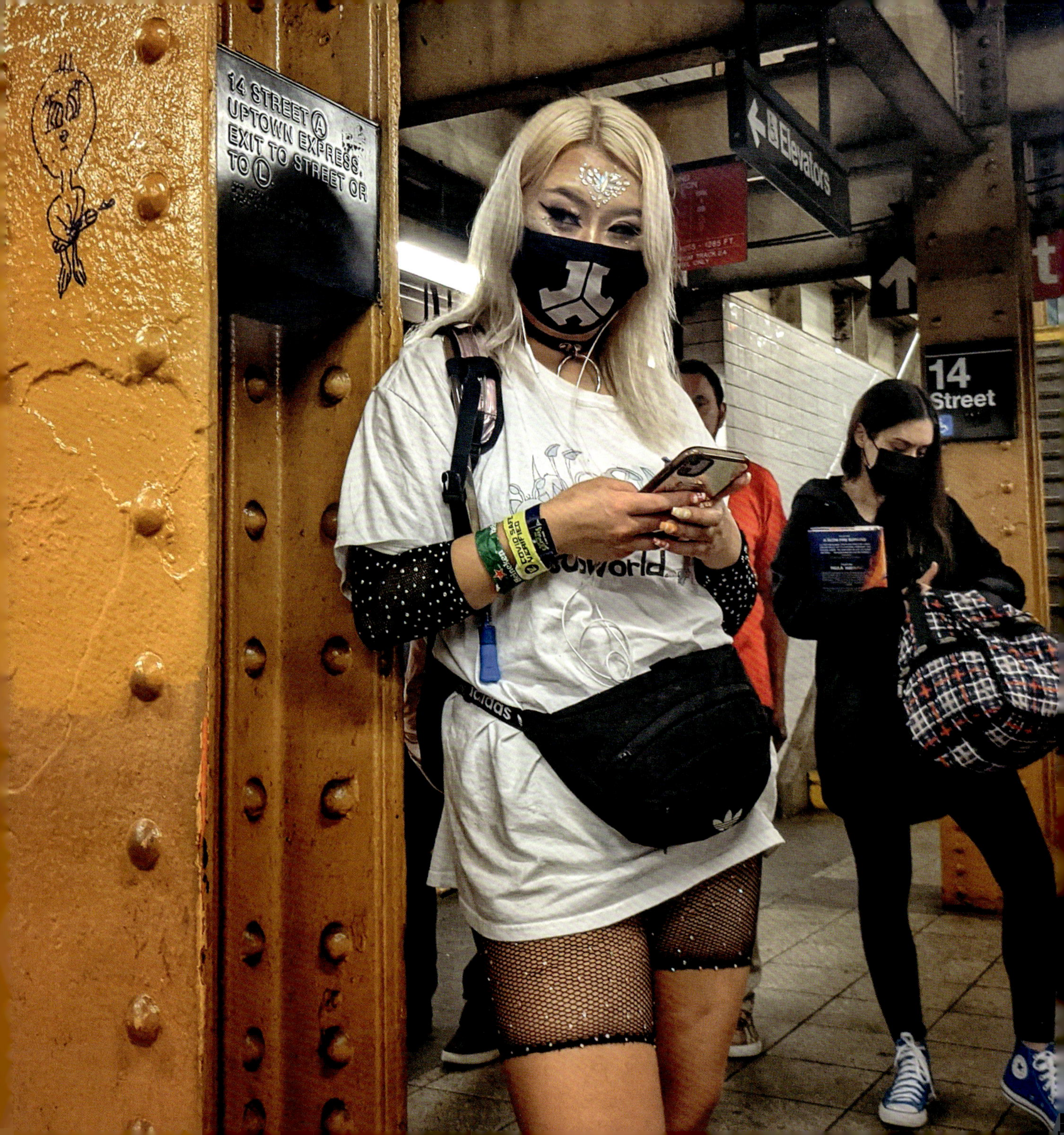

14 STREET Ⓐ
UPTOWN EXPRESS
EXIT TO STREET OR
TO Ⓛ
Elevators
14
Street

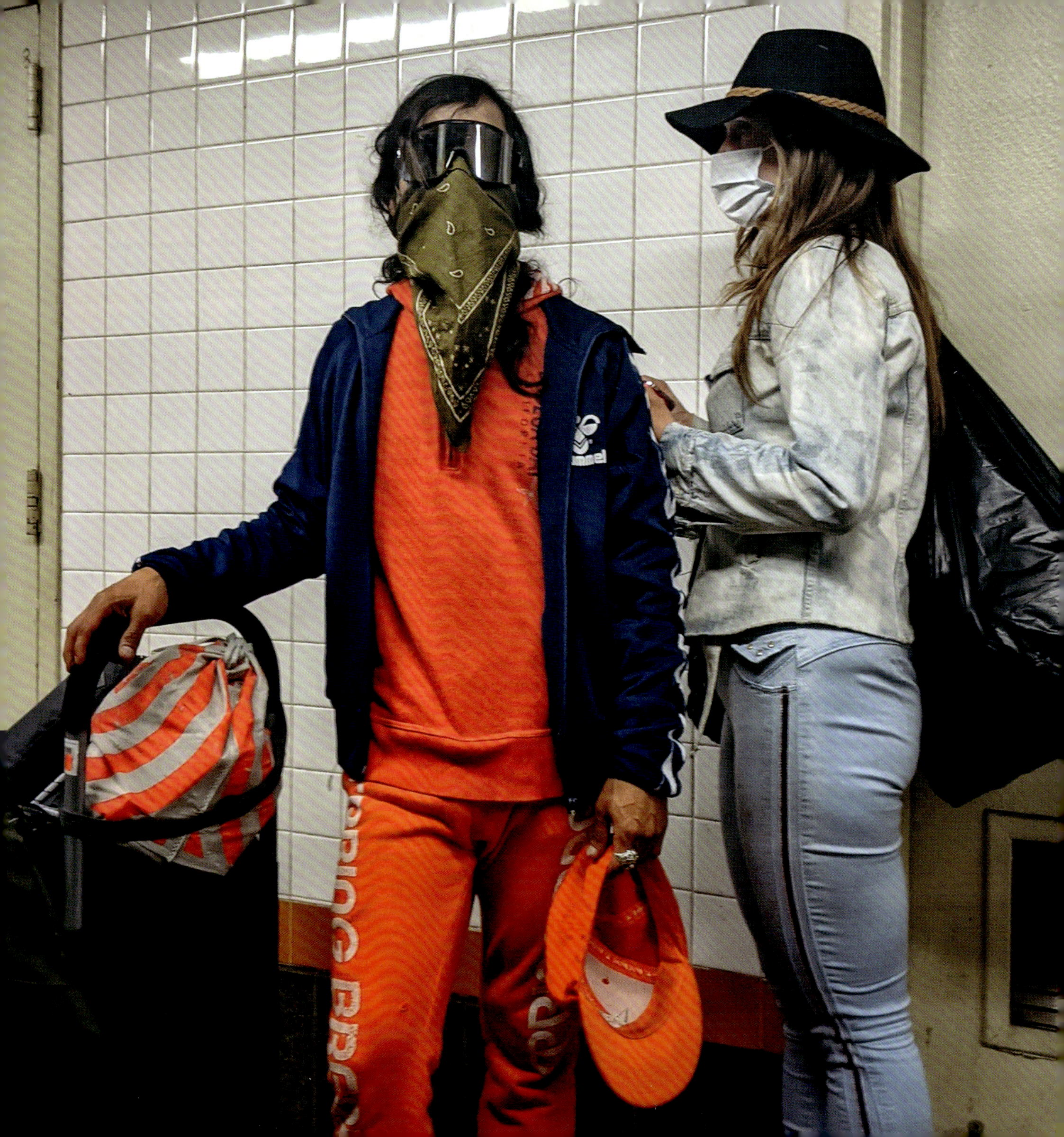

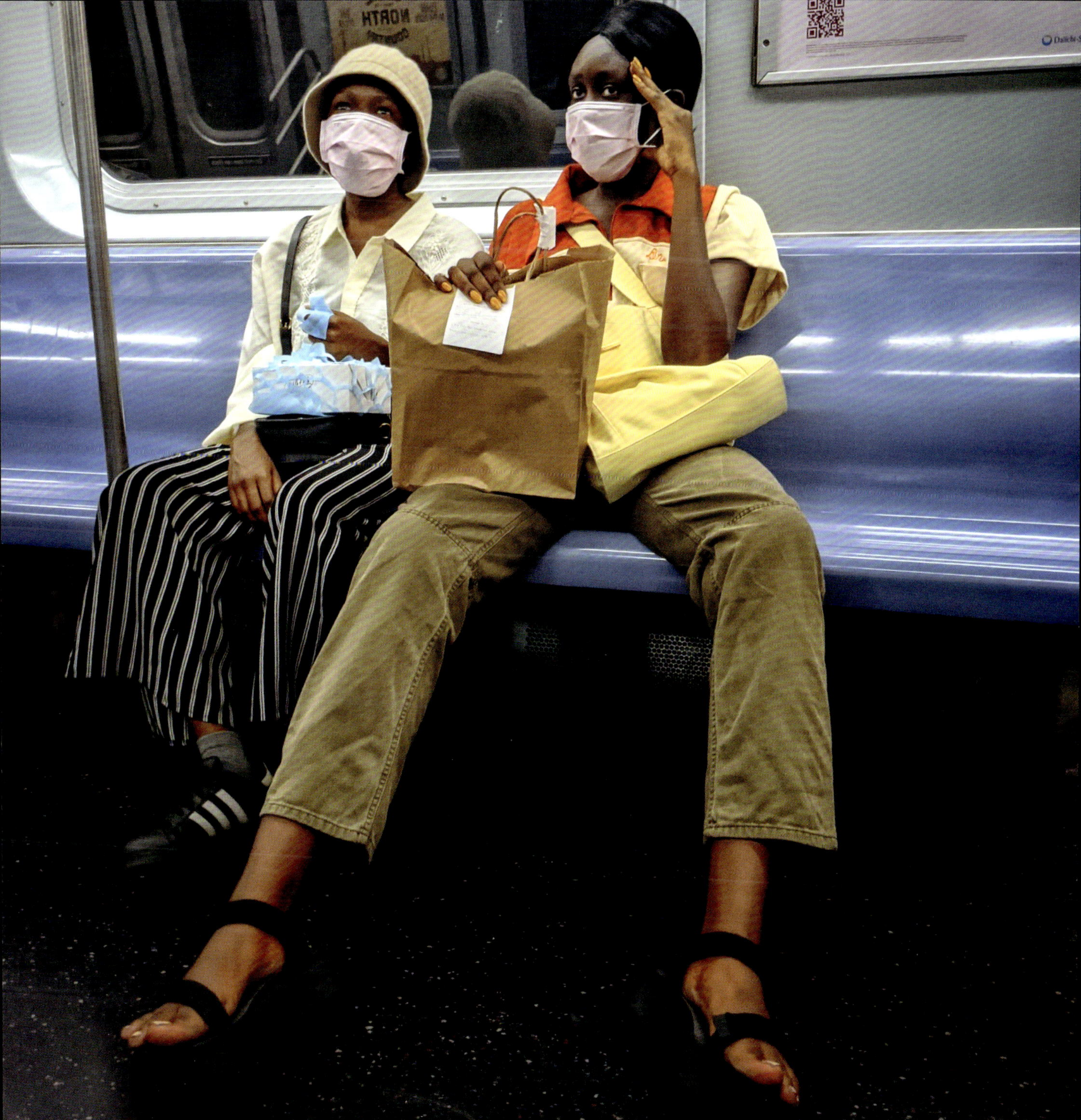

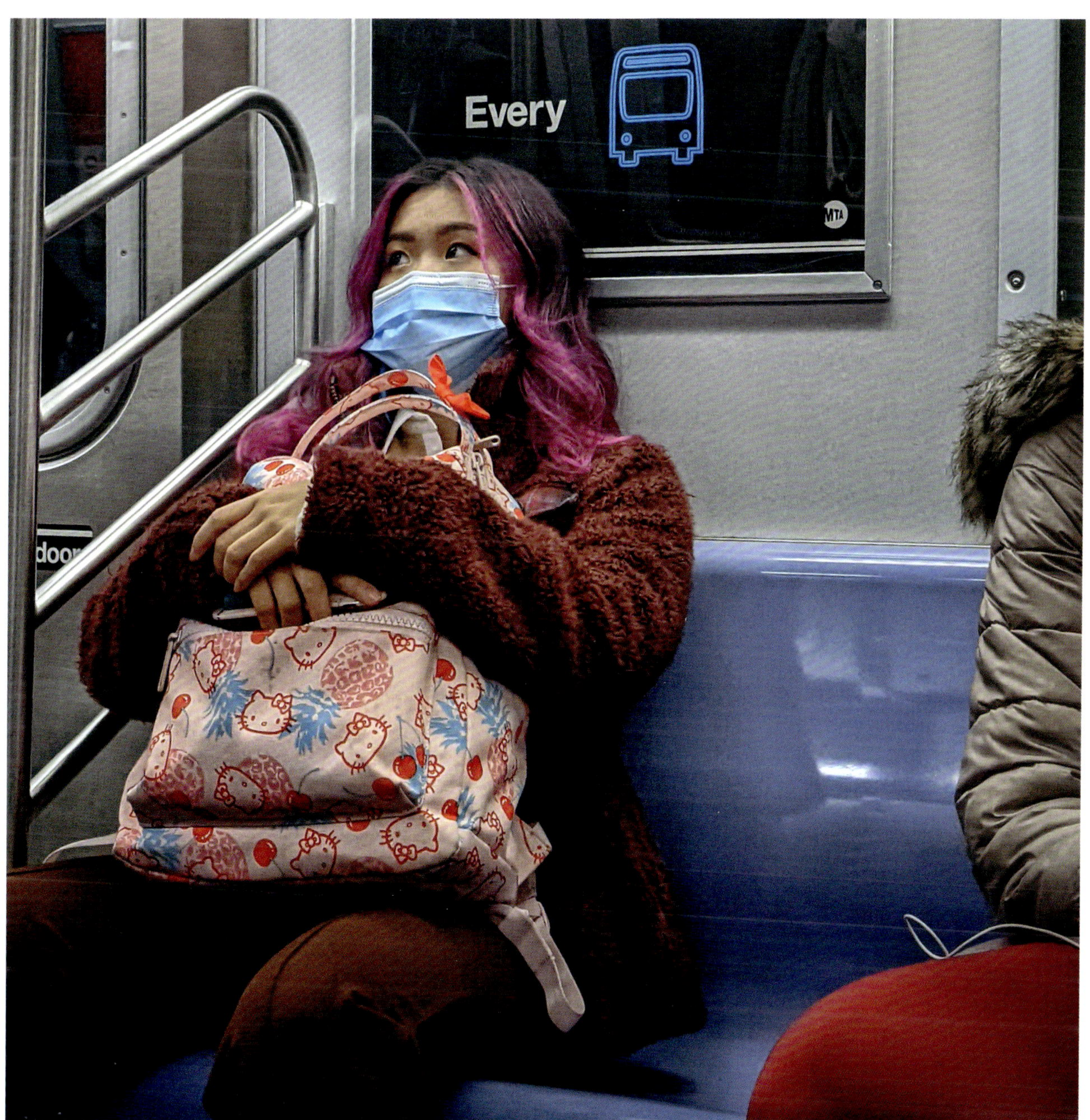

Every
MTA
door

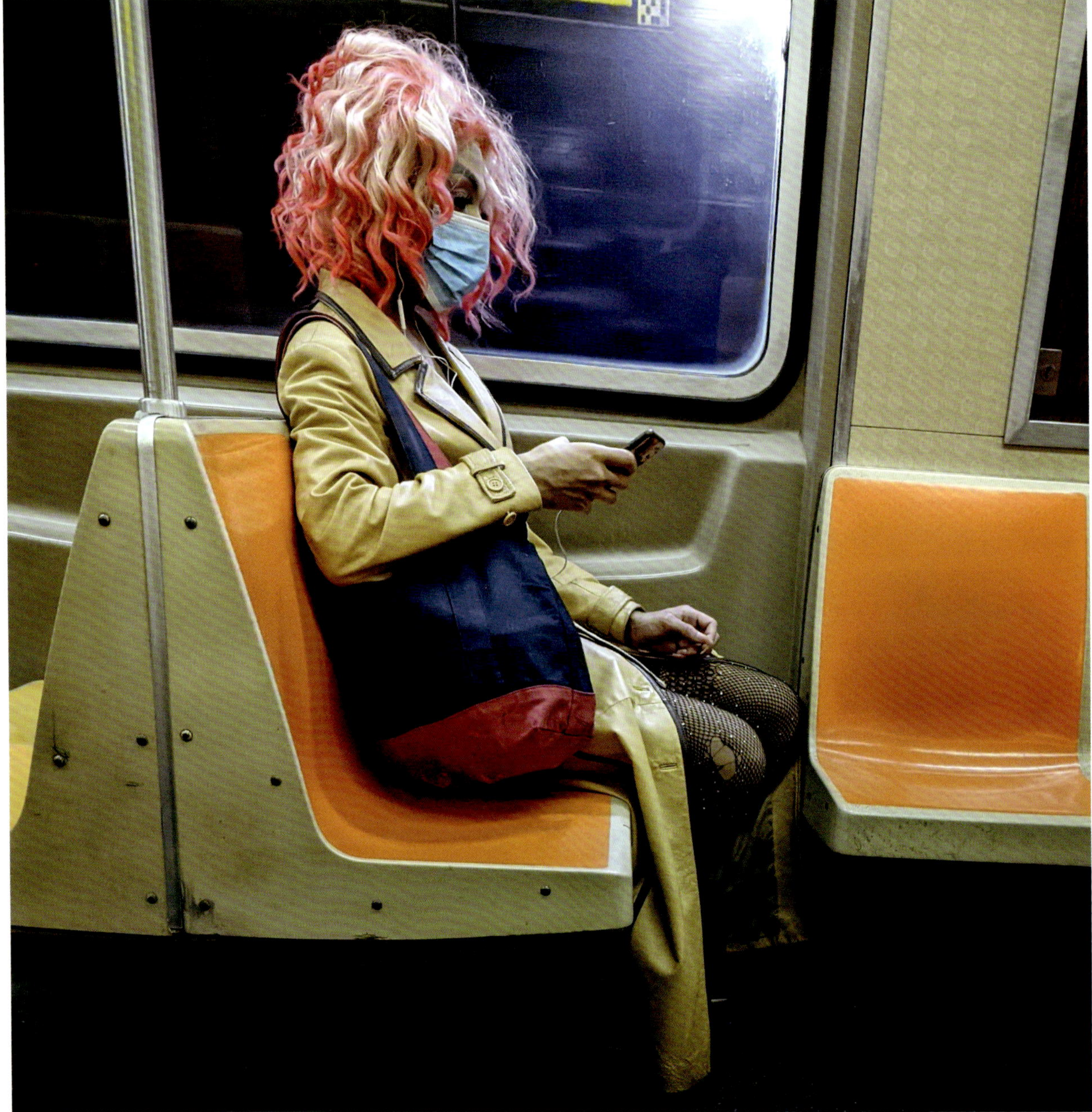

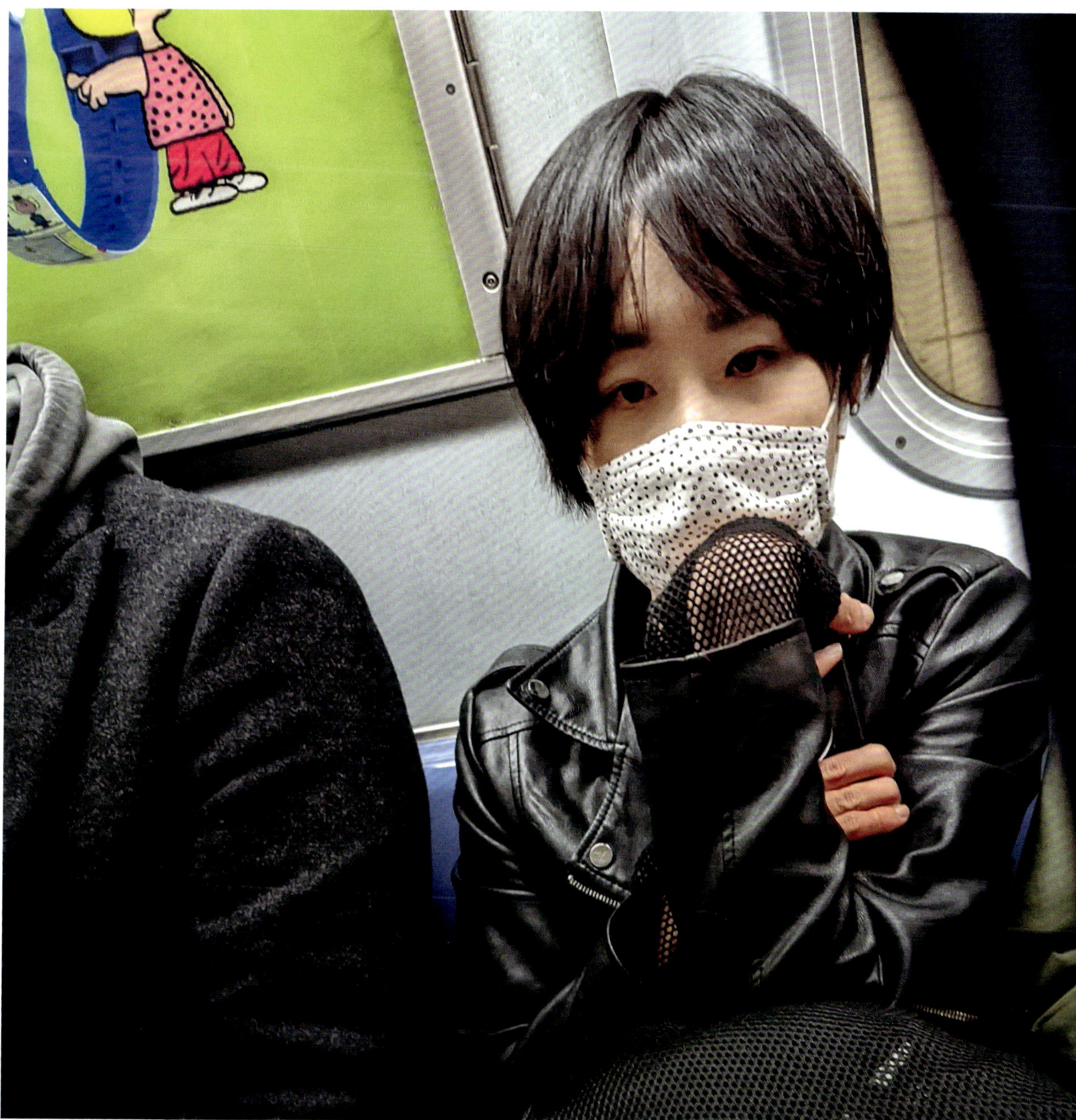

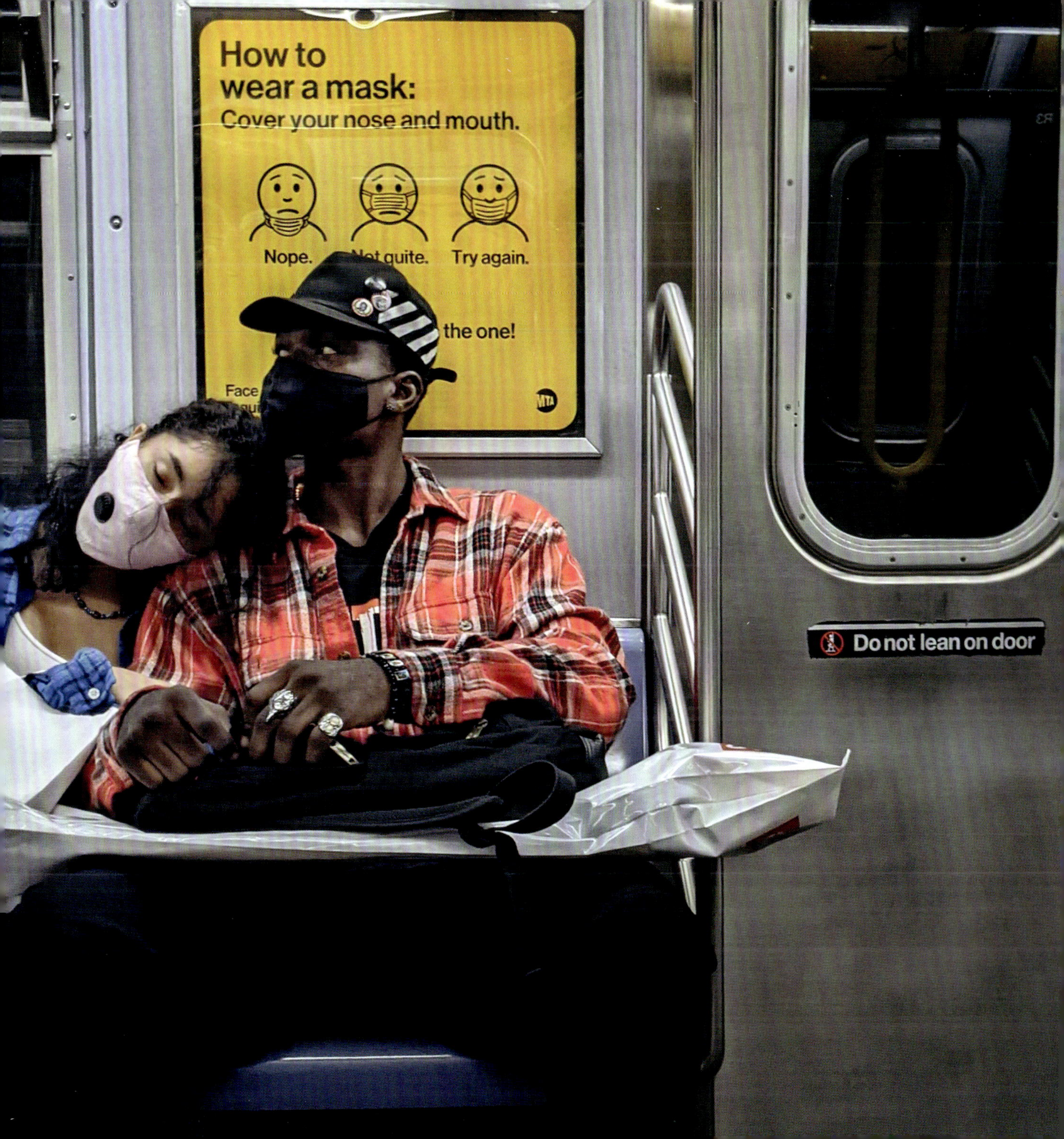

How to
wear a mask:
Cover your nose and mouth.
Nope.   Not quite.   Try again.
the one!
Face
MTA
Do not lean on door

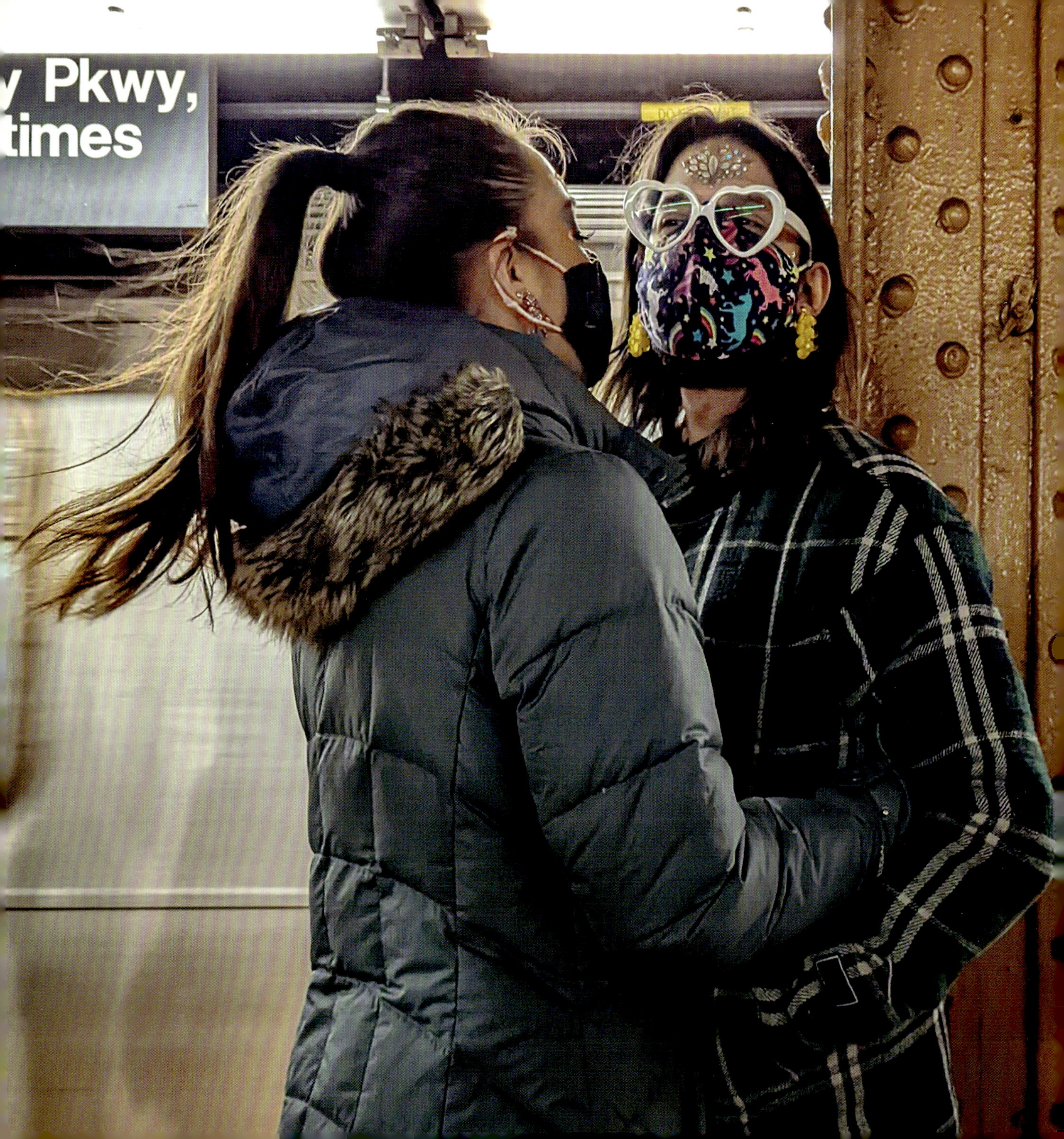
y Pkwy,
times

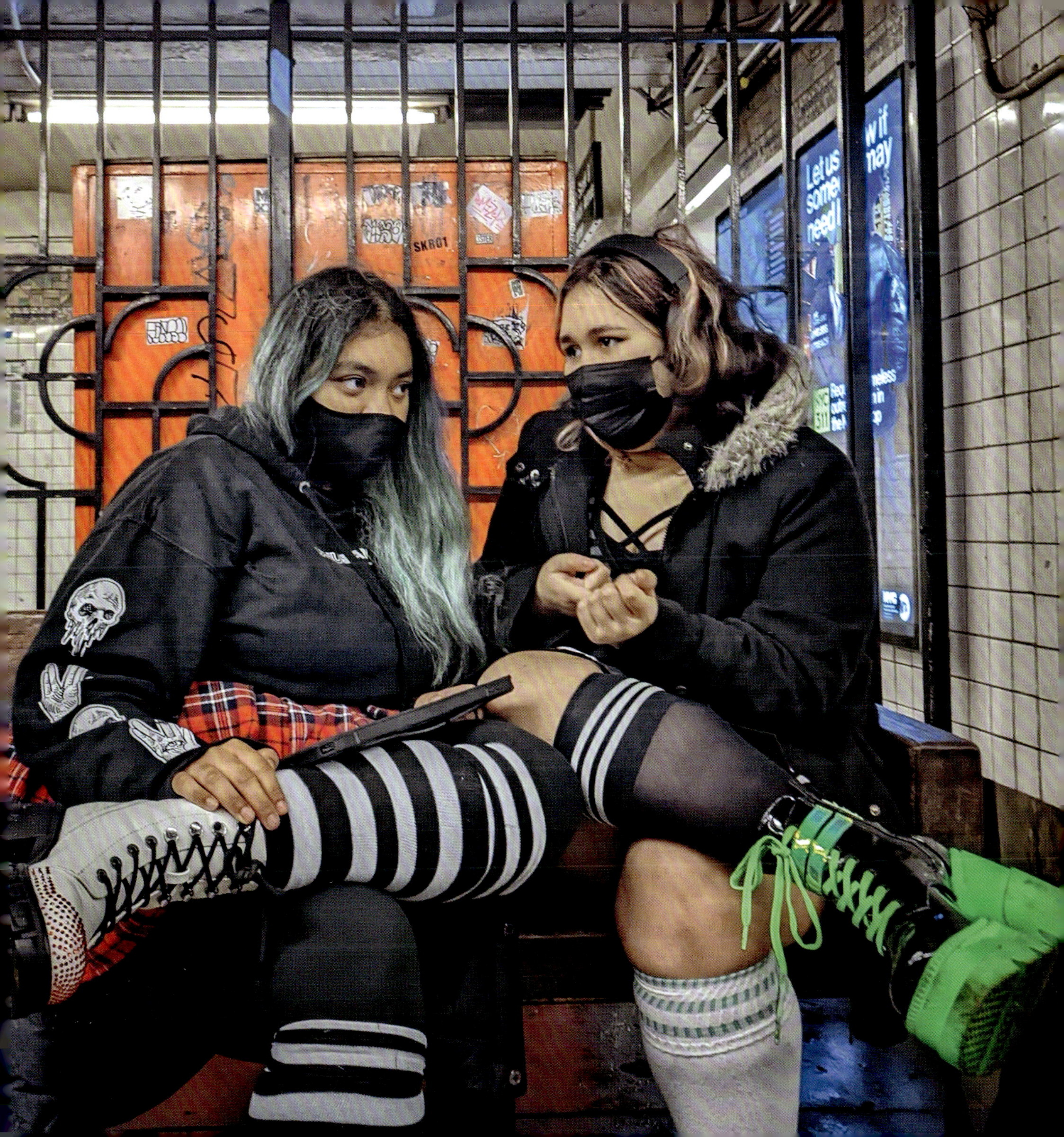

SKR01
Let us
some
need
W if
nay
less
in
p

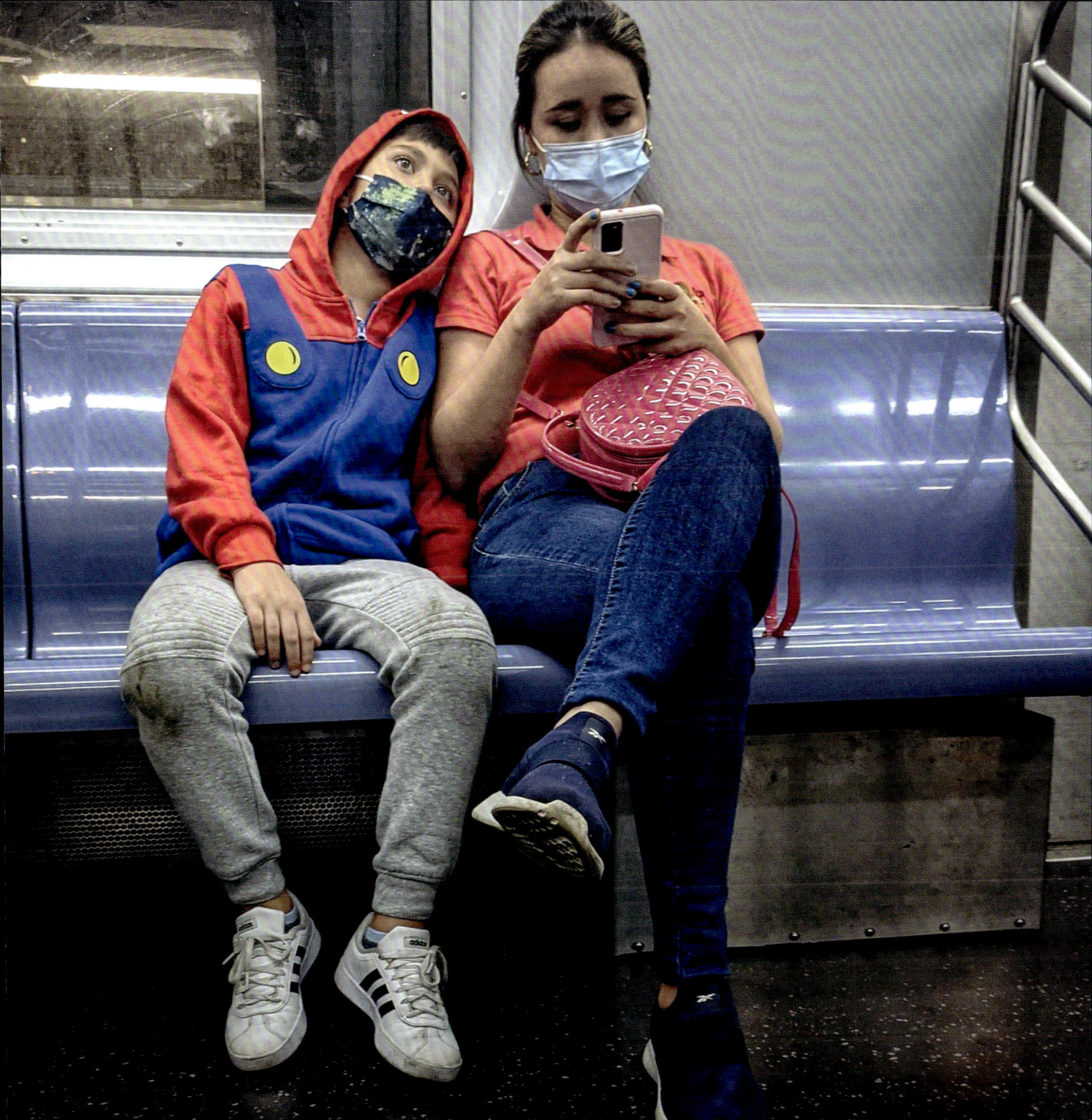

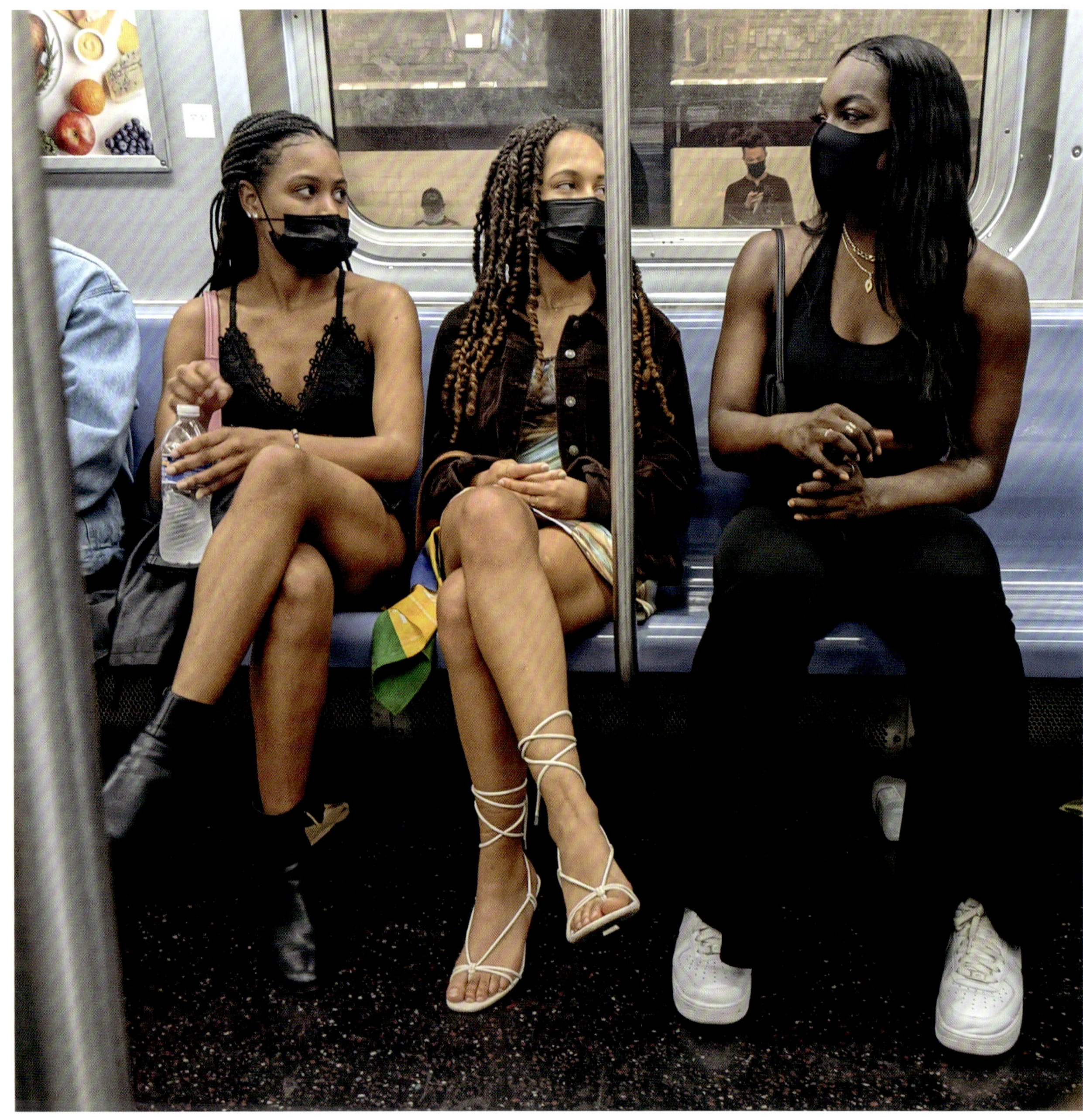

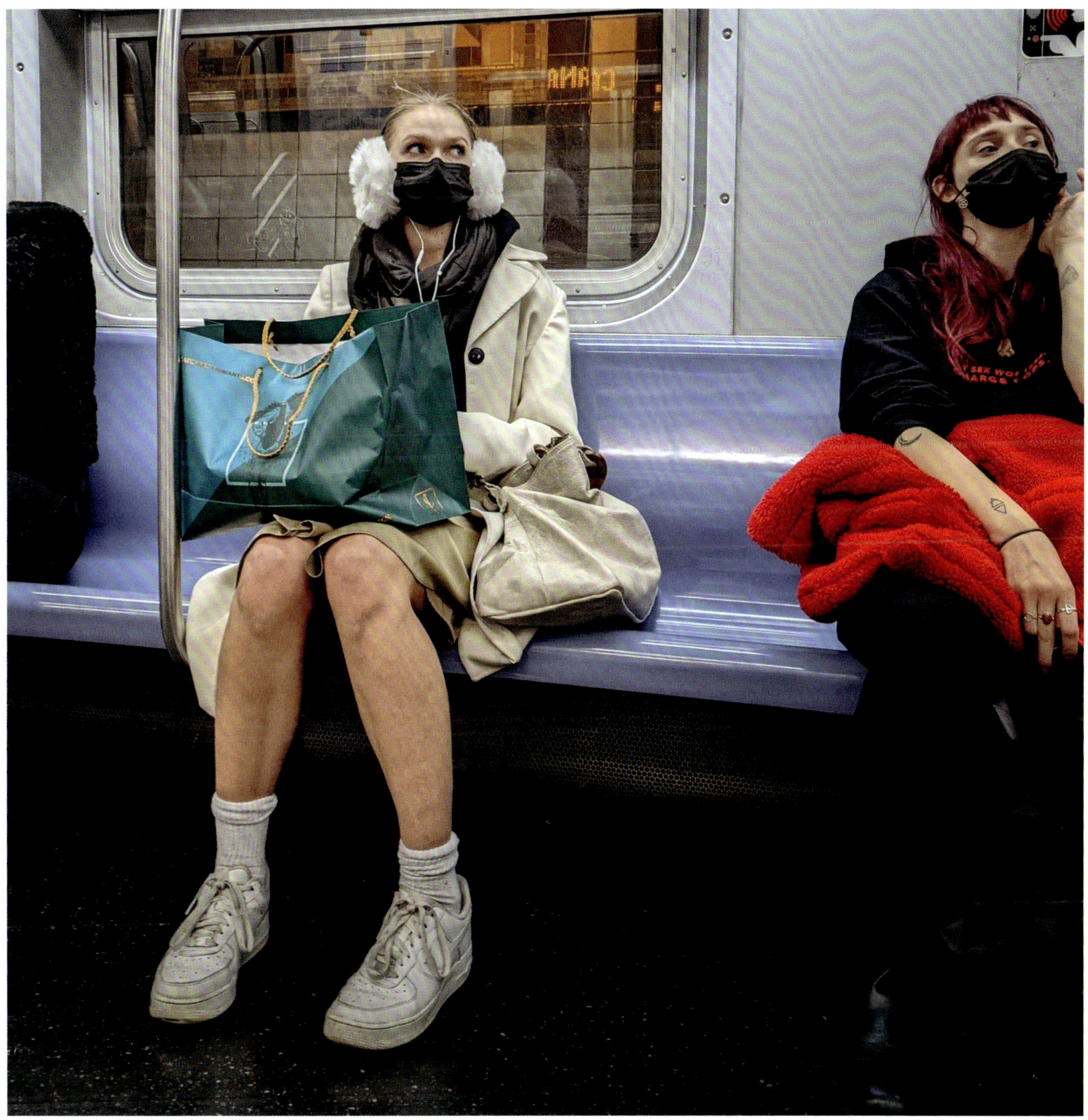

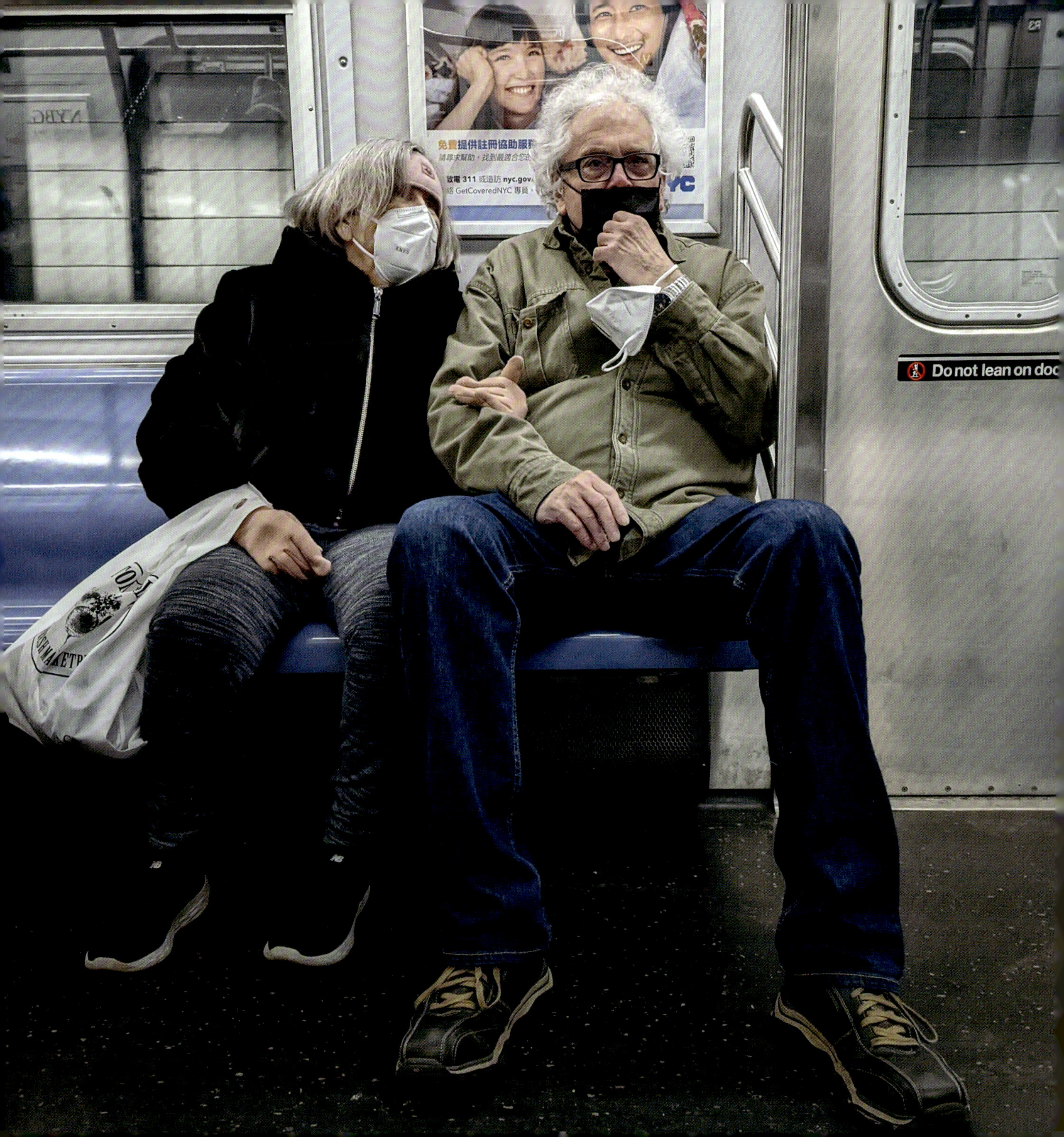

免費提供註冊協助服
請尋求幫助，找到最適合您的
致電 311 或造訪 nyc.gov
絡 GetCoveredNYC 專員
NYC
Do not lean on doo

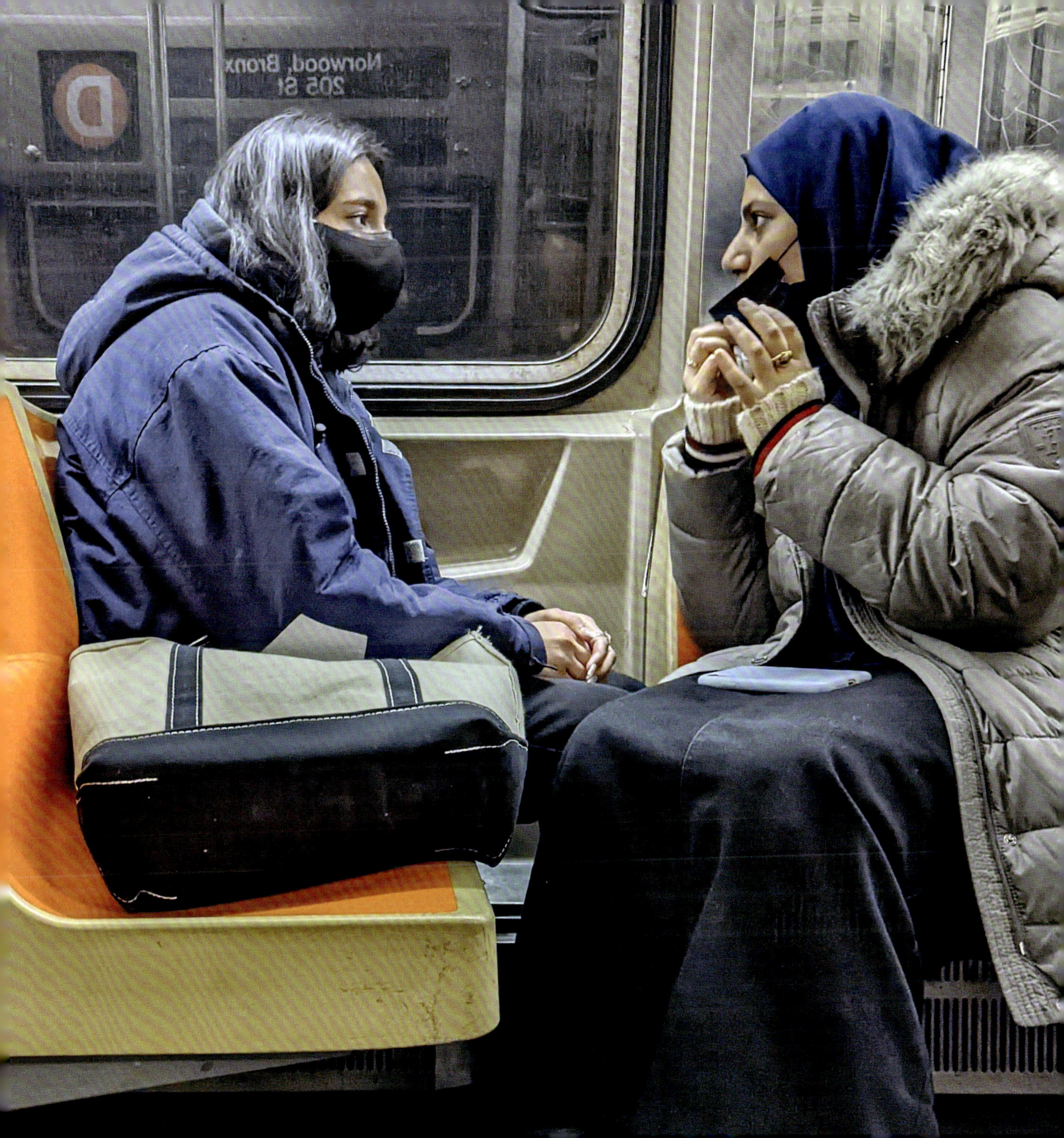

Norwood, Bronx
205 St

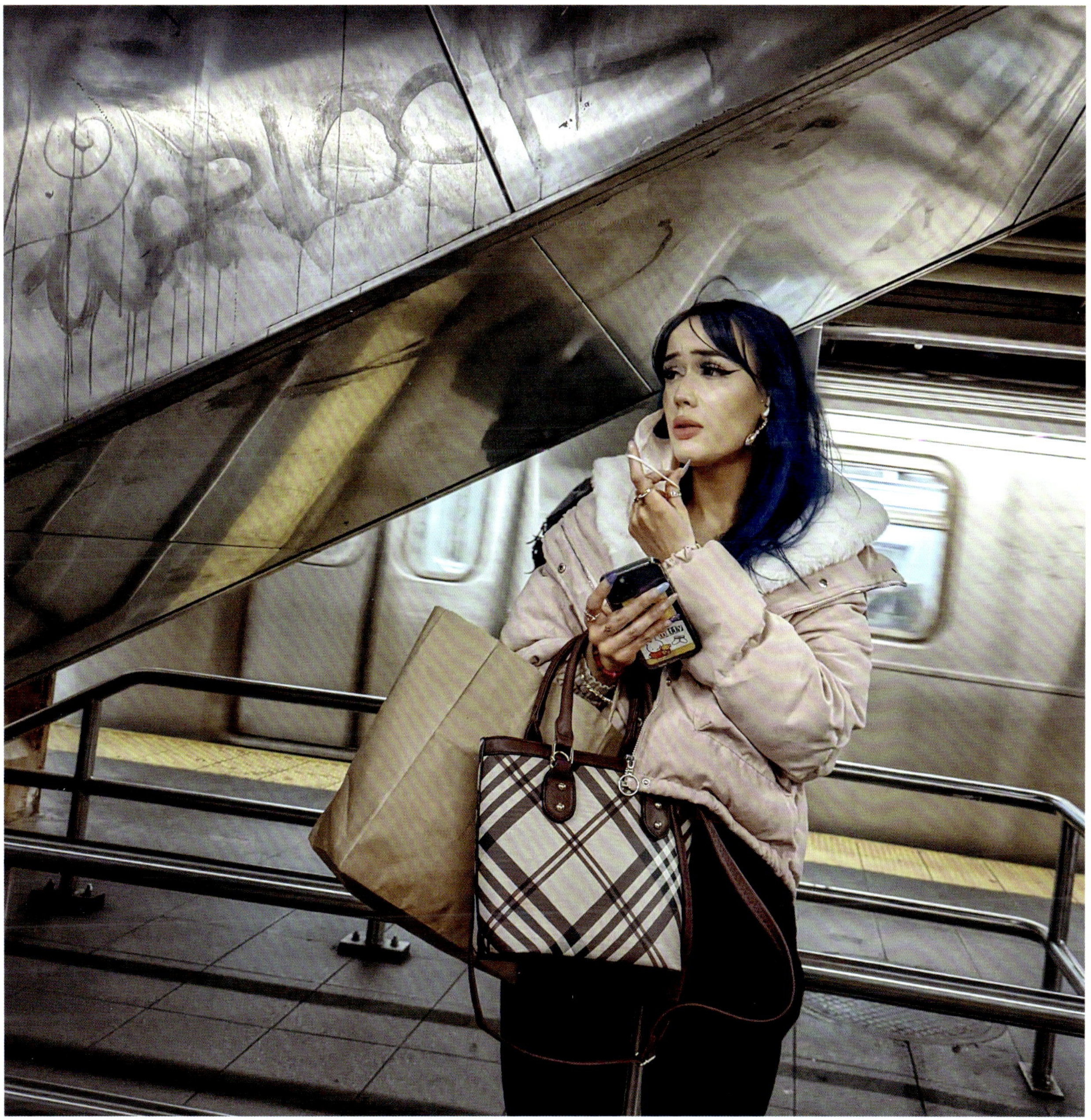

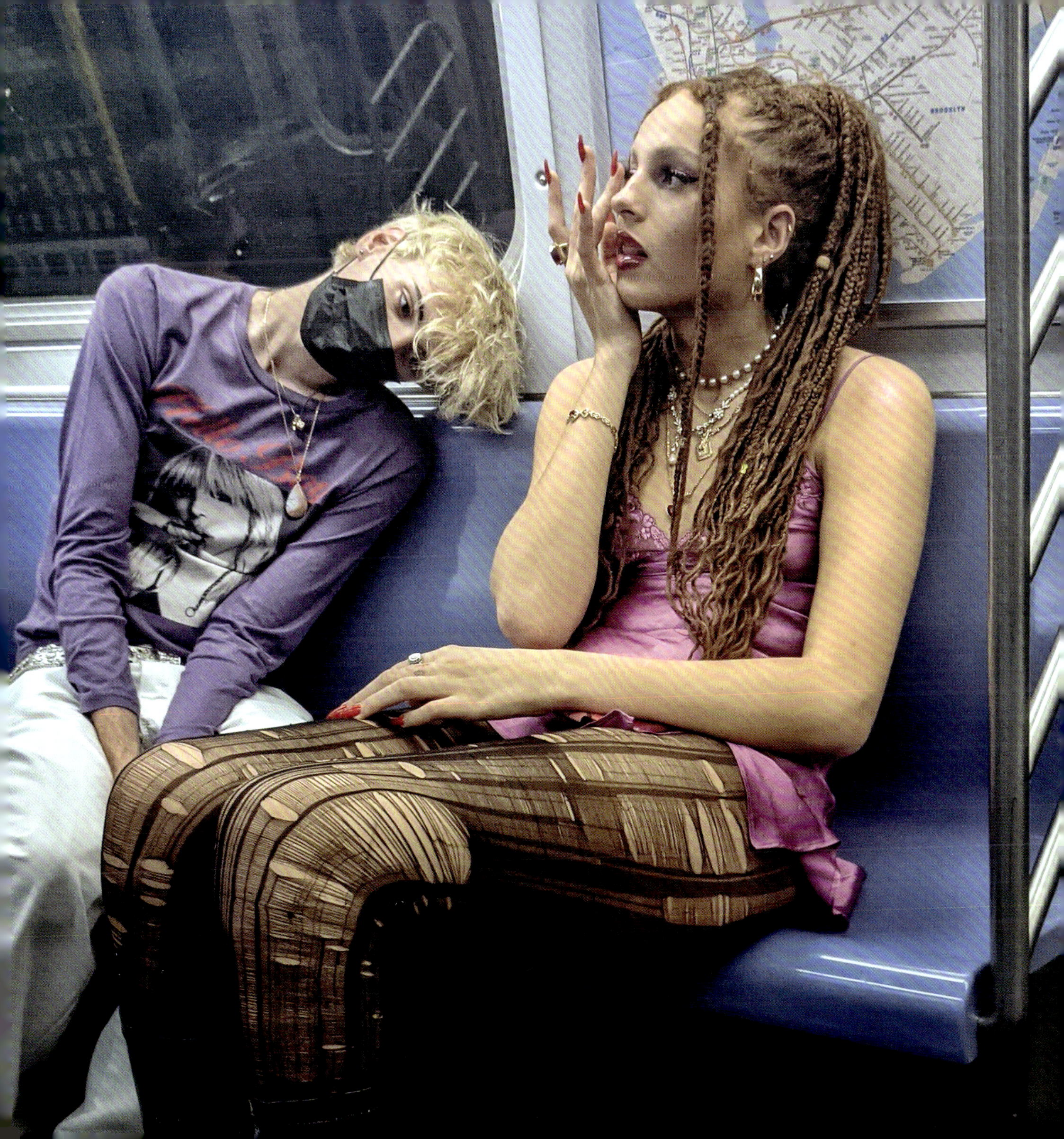

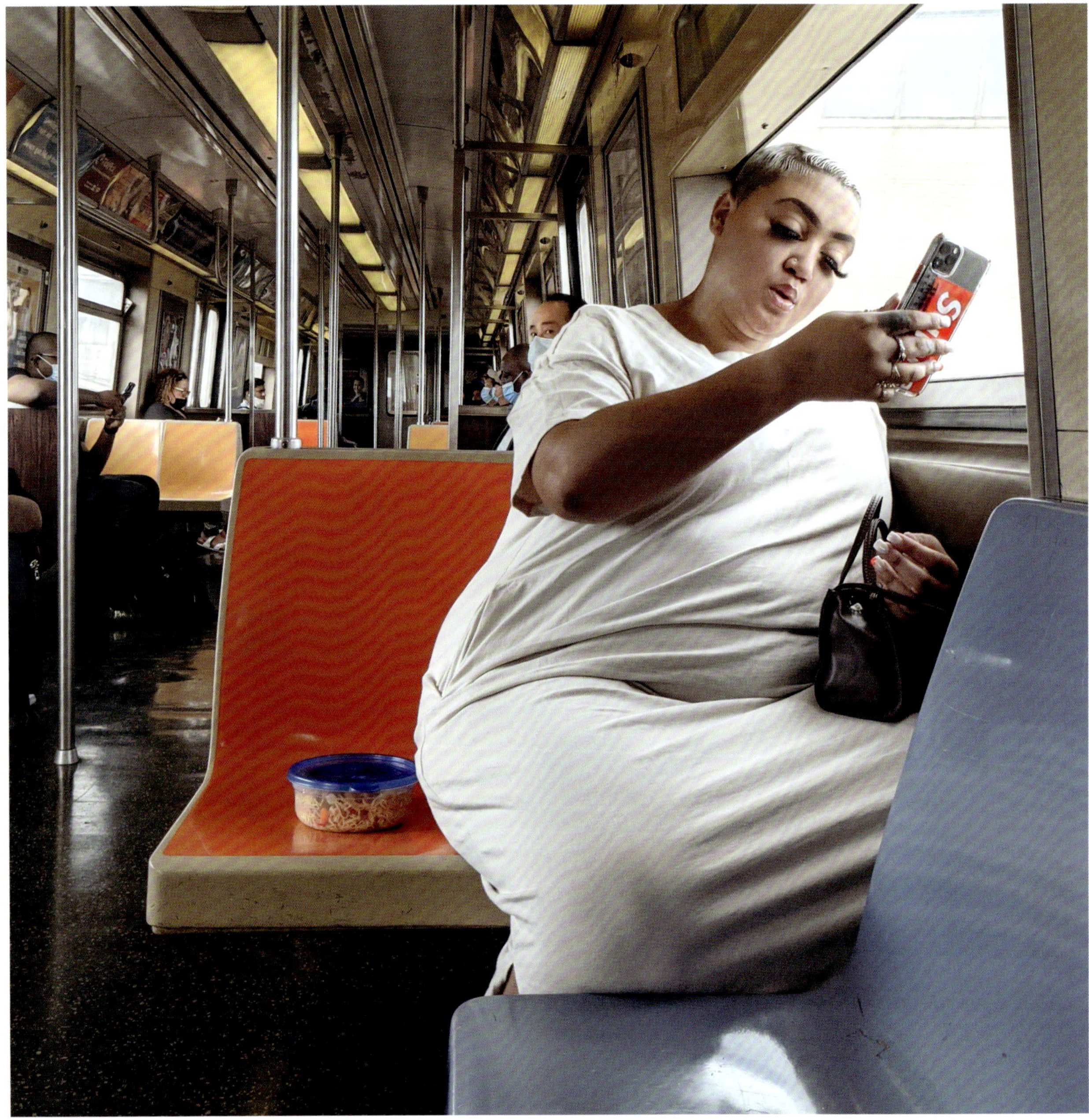

STEADFAST

by Aaron L. Morrison

For a system older than the Spanish flu, the last pandemic to leave an unfathomable amount of human destruction in its wake, New York City's subway may be the world's most indelible public resource.

With very few interruptions, it deposits and disburses humanity. Through plague, natural disaster, and man-made calamity, the system was designed to be steadfast and resolute in its purpose.

Boosters and hustlers. Evangelists and doomsdayers. Abusers and shooters. Whoever may lurk on its platforms, the subway's trains arrive, open up, and issue polite instruction.

Stand clear of the closing doors, please.

Of course, the subway and its devotees are just as capable of spreading joy and hope as they are of triggering our anxiety and fears. The smile that spreads across our faces, masked or unmasked, when a father lovingly occupies the attention of his adorably dressed daughters until they can reach their destination. The second-hand confidence we feel when a fellow rider was meticulous in assembling that night-out ensemble.

And there are the laughs we get, the ones that momentarily pierce through our worries. The giggle that we have to stifle when we realize we're sitting across from a bearded dragon that has its own luxurious carrier. The way we can't wait to get above ground to tell someone about the Sailor Moon character sandwiched between two men who appear slovenly in comparison.

A safe ride for many of us requires a kind of hypnosis, a mental pendulum swinging between a state of daydream and alertness. That hypnosis makes almost bearable the forced physical closeness, the delays, or the bellowed sermons and "showtime" performances from which there seems no escape.

We're our truest self in the subway. The system unmasks riders without removing face coverings, often with indifference.

It reveals the predators, the self-absorbed, and the bigots. It calls out to activists, first responders, and good Samaritans. And it watches as riders straddle the line of good and evil, measuring how brotherly we'll be to each other in the short time that we must share space.

We'll all get to where we're going, even when the destination is unknown. We'll endure.

Do not hold the doors.

This collection of images—moments that are otherwise blips in the expansive history of New York's public transit system—shows how humanity grapples with daily life, unaware of what the ride has in store.

Yes, the coronavirus pandemic of 2020 greatly altered our existence. But the subway has to be impervious in the ways that humans are not.

For that reason, Chris Maliwat's *Subwaygram* is prescient and a rare body of work. A historical record, a testimony of our values, a parable of inequality. Moments worth preserving and studying.

Maliwat wasn't a safarist or an outside observer. A faithful subway rider himself, Maliwat bore witness to what most would otherwise miss in their routine commutes to work and back home. He told me the work was meditative—a way of working through his own anxieties and finding commonality with fellow riders.

For two years before the pandemic, Maliwat documented the spectrum between self-consciousness and unselfconsciousness: The "fair lady" seated with a glorious red crown of hair, eyes hidden by sunglasses with American flag frames. The couples seen in mid-embrace, perhaps their first or their last.

Do you love me? Am I cared for? Are you with me? Will you help me?

And for two years after the onset of the pandemic, Maliwat documented cautiousness and uncertainty: The woman seated below a public health warning, her eyes seeming to search for reassurance. The Black man found resting his eyes and wearing a "Stop killing us" mask, a message and desperate plea of the times.

I love you. I care about you. I'm with you. We'll do this together.

The system has had to carry on because many of its riders do, too. When millions stayed home, walled off from the lurking virus, classes of working people weren't afforded that same choice.

The shelf stockers, cooks, deliverers, and dashers. Innumerable categories of people for whom the subway is a lifeline.

The system also became treacherous for Asian New Yorkers, whether they were citizens, immigrants, or visitors. As some sought to place blame for the arrival of coronavirus, people of Chinese descent and other Asian identities faced an unrelenting barrage of hate and unprovoked attacks.

More than a year into the pandemic, Michelle Alyssa Go, a forty-year-old Asian American woman, was pushed in front of a Manhattan subway train to her death. Impacted communities banded together to fund taxi fare for riders who felt unsafe in that climate.

There is no vaccine for hatred and xenophobia, so we subway passengers must not look the other way in the face of such inhumanity. Morally, a riders' fare must be higher.

Much like the image of the woman wearing all white signals (her seatmate is a container of pasta salad), a new normal will always emerge after periods of turmoil. But what lies ahead isn't necessarily a rebirth.

The subway will continue pulling in, opening up, and giving polite instruction. But it is not the system that is steadfast and resolute on its own. It is we who must be those things.

PLATELIST

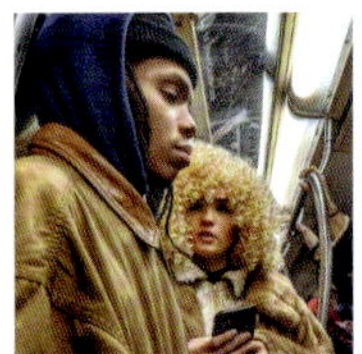

#blondambition
February 2020

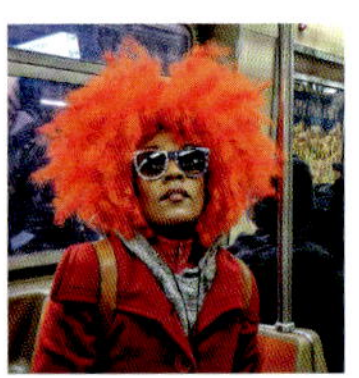

#myfairlady
January 2019

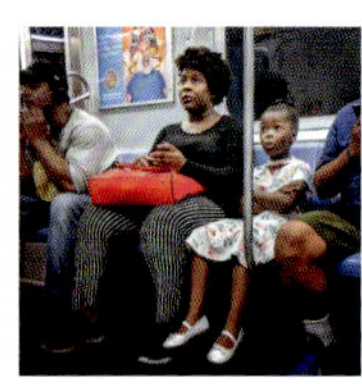

😆😳😮
September 2018

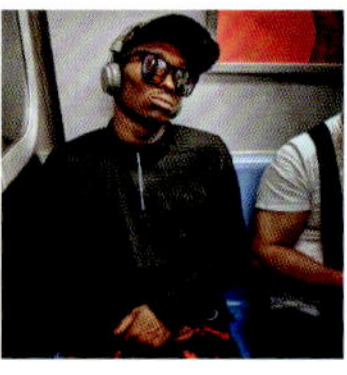

🎧 👓
September 2018

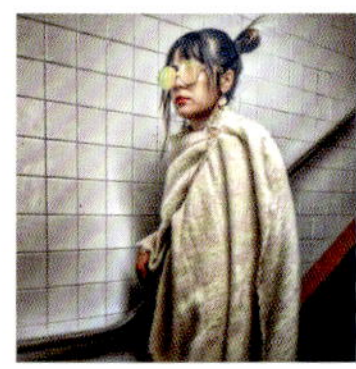

👓
November 2018

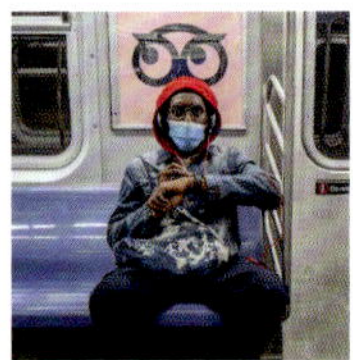

#who
October 2020

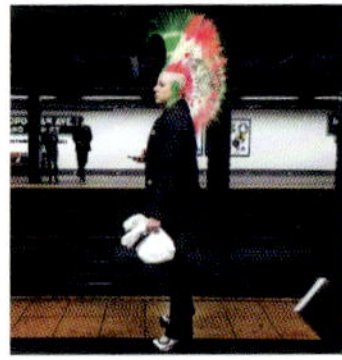

#cockadoo
October 2014

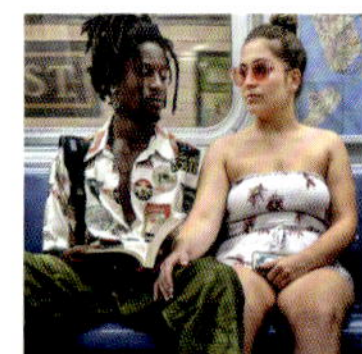

#coupling
July 2019

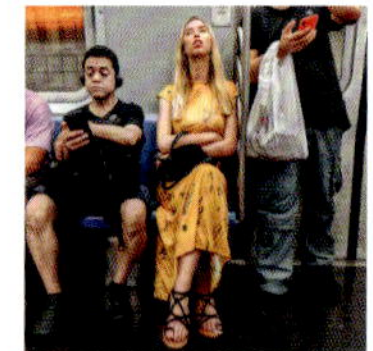

#waitforsteadylight
August 2018

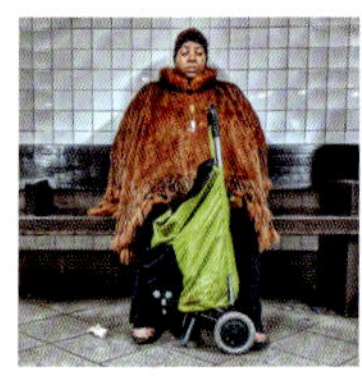

❄❄❄
November 2018

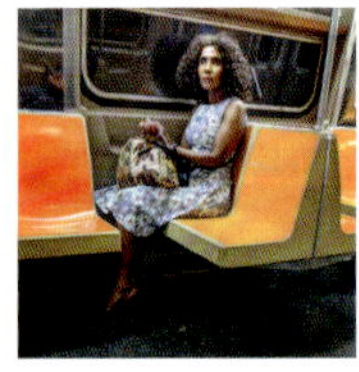

#turtlesandflowers
July 2018

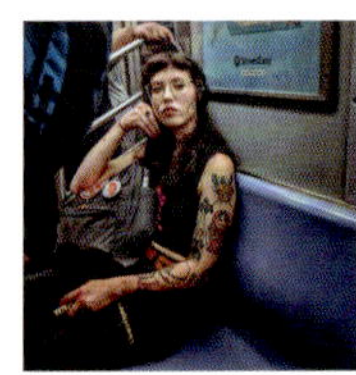

#femaletrouble
July 2018

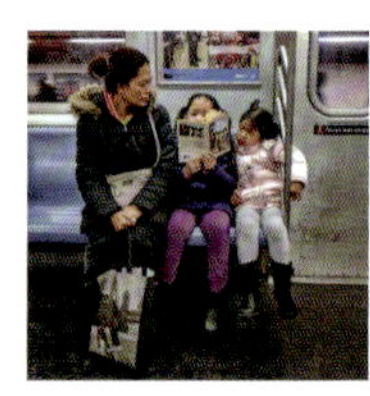

#readingisfundamental
January 2017

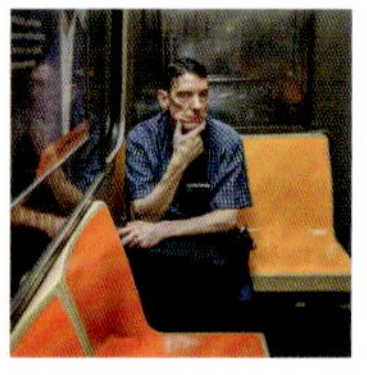

#turnthatfrownupsidedown
September 2019

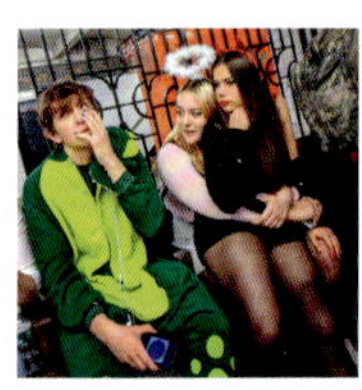

#eyeopening
October 2019

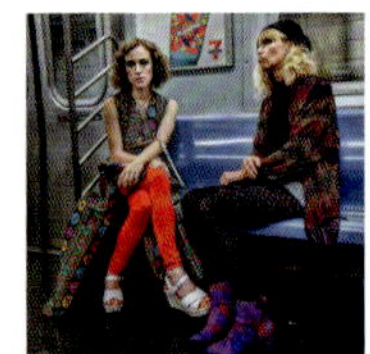

#slurpees
August 2018

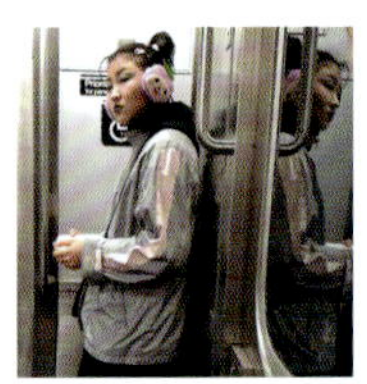

#muffs
February 2019

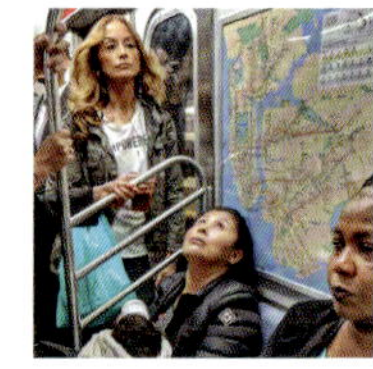

#empowered
October 2018

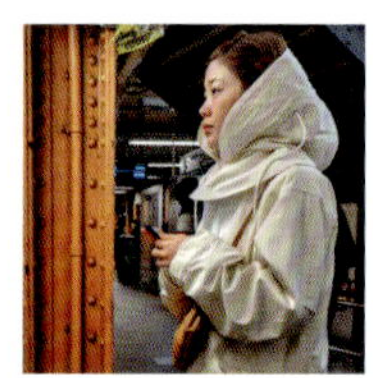

#caution
April 2019

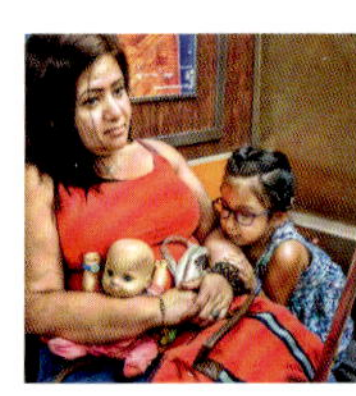

🌼
September 2018

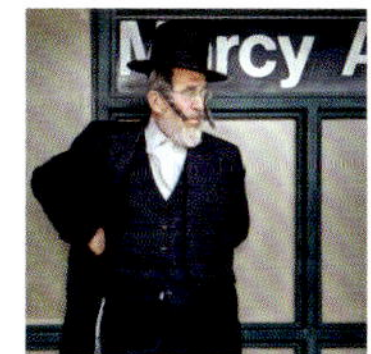

#sway
October 2018

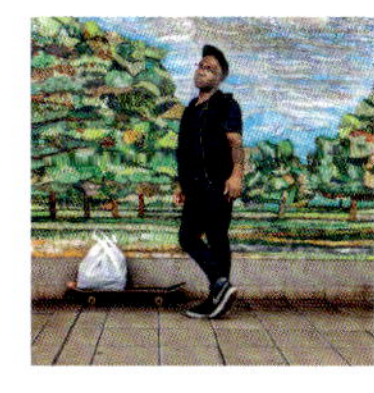

#🌳🌳🌳🌳🌳🏃🌳🌳
August 2018

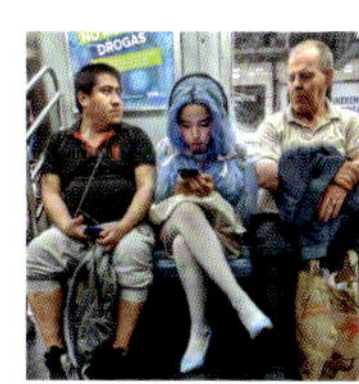

#movie
June 2019

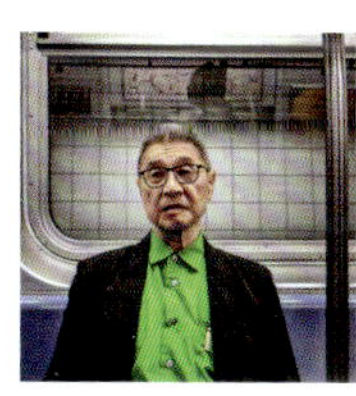

#itsnoteasy
October 2018

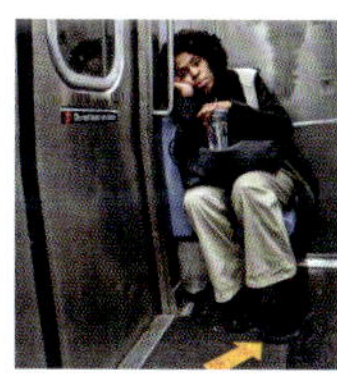

#upandtotheright
January 2019

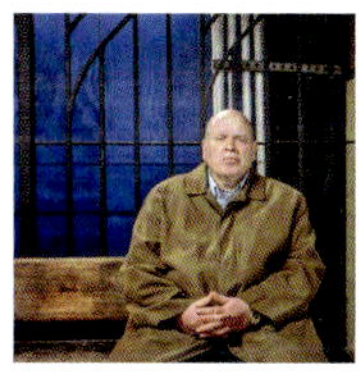

#blueline
November 2018

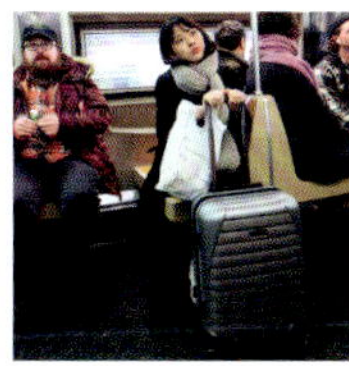

#wanderlust
February 2017

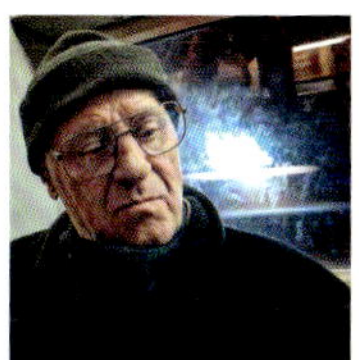

#starbright
December 2018

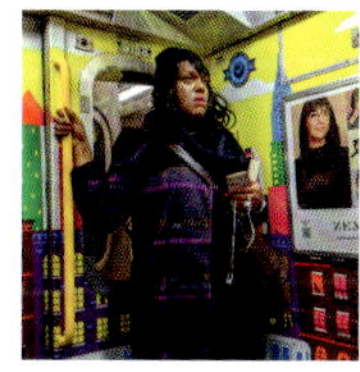

#zen
December 2019

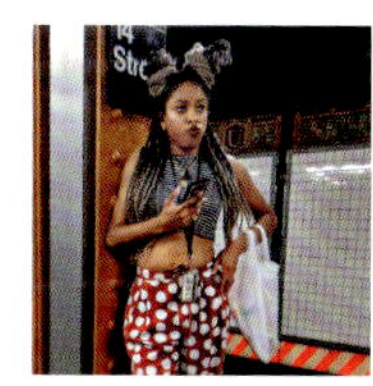

#BeU
June 2019

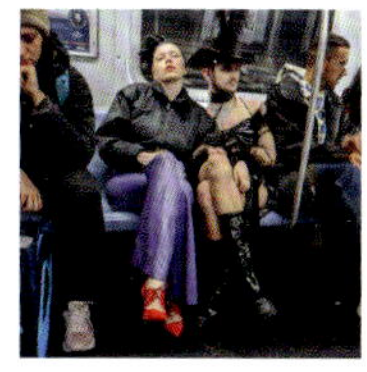

#LTrainOrHalloween
November 2019

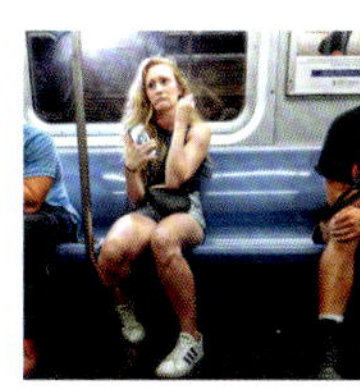

#hairraising
July 2018

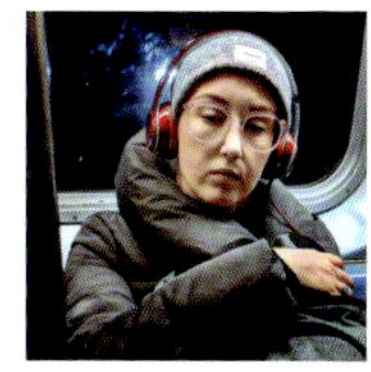

#beats
January 2019

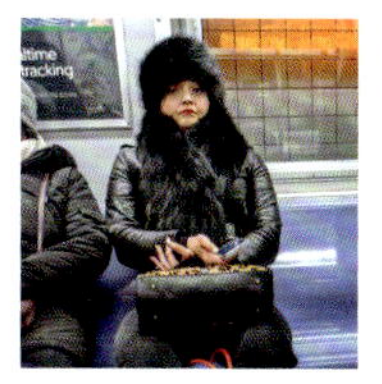

#tracking
February 2020

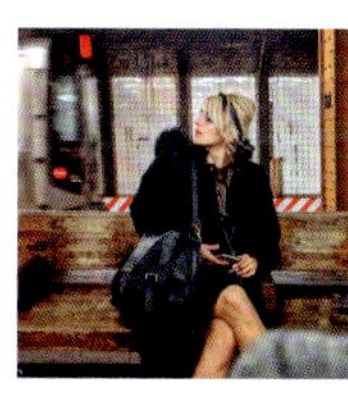

#brooklynbound
November 2018

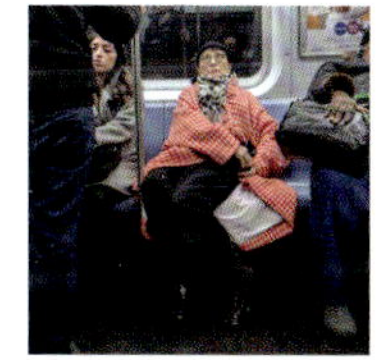

#checksandbalances
January 2017

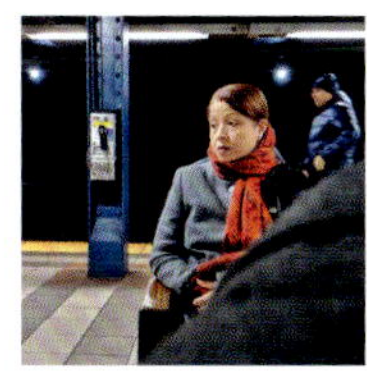

#hello
December 2018

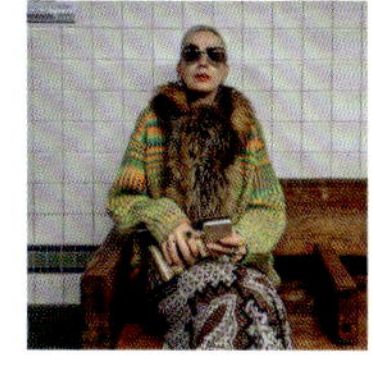

#patterns
November 2019

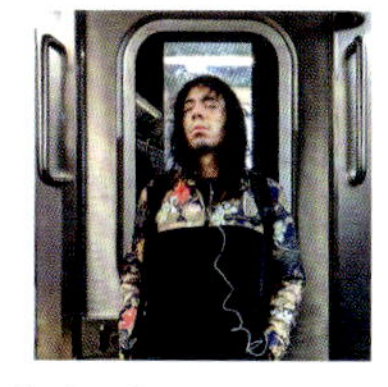

#wired
November 2018

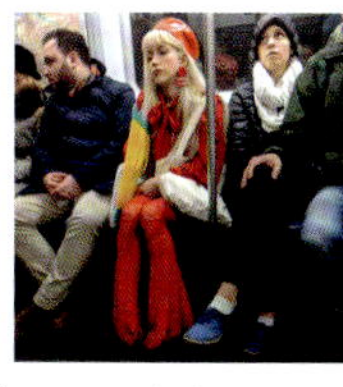

#merrychristmas
December 2018

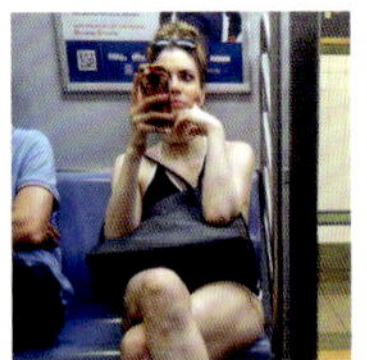

#tigereyes
June 2019

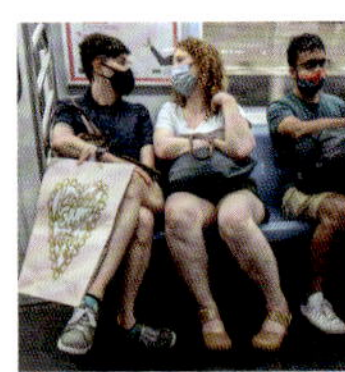

#happilyeverafter
September 2021

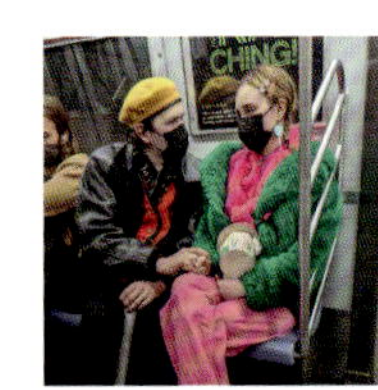

#take12
March 2022

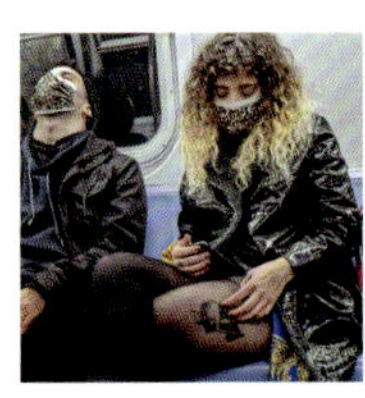

#takestwototango
December 2021

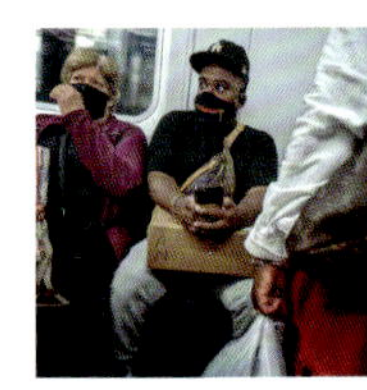

#unzipped
September 2021

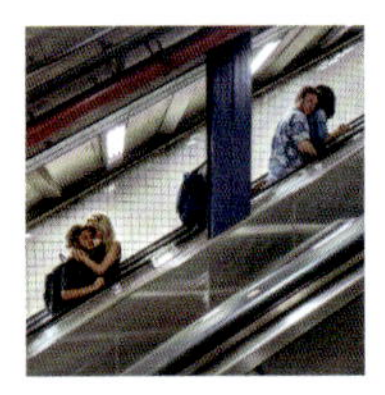

#behindeverywoman
October 2019

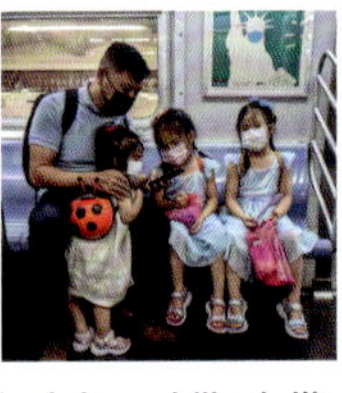

#ladybug / #ladyliberty
September 2021

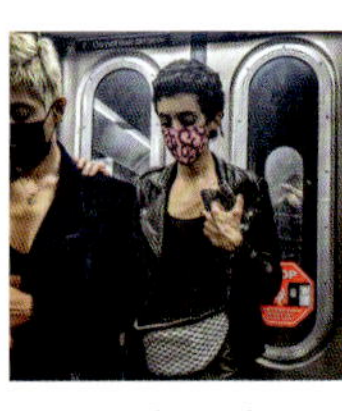

#putyourhandonmy
shoulder
July 2018

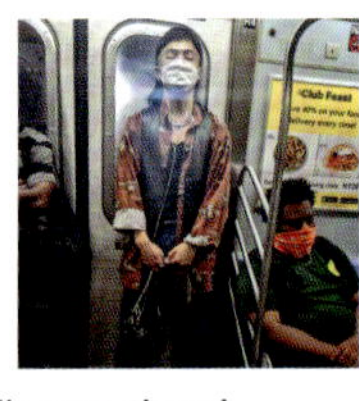

#everytime!
November 2021

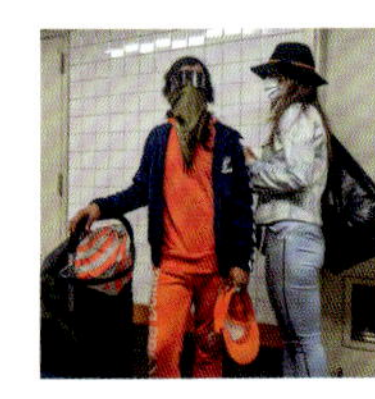

#target
November 2021

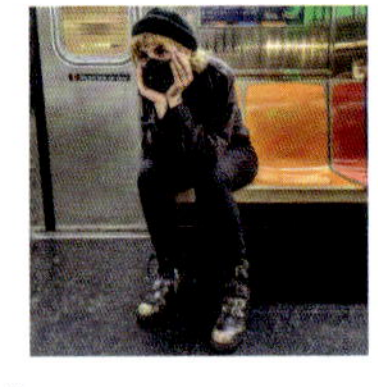

#nyccares
October 2021

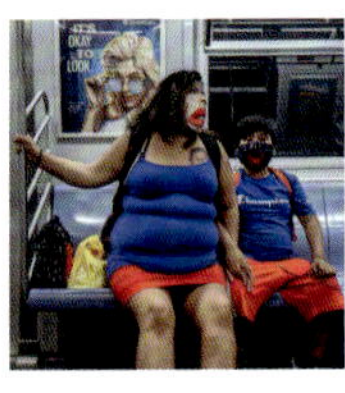

#itsoktolook
August 2020

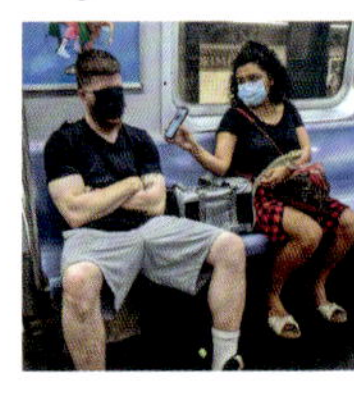

#seenoevil
August 2021

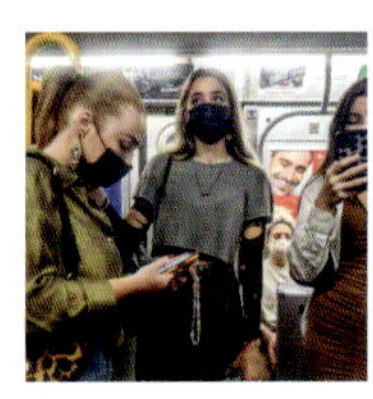

#itsneveronlyadream
December 2021

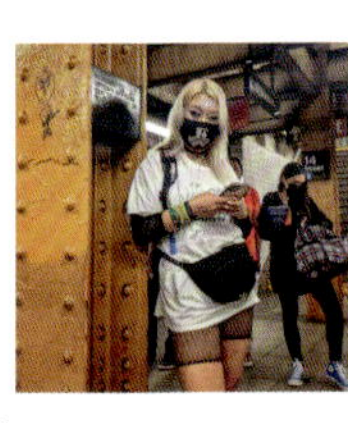

#uptownexpress
October 2021

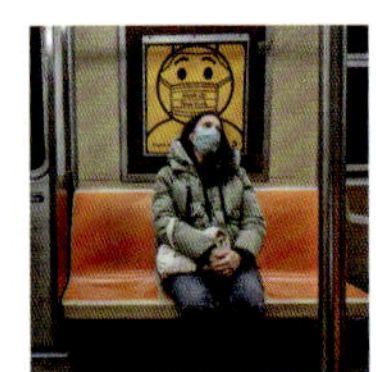

#maskupnewyork
November 2021

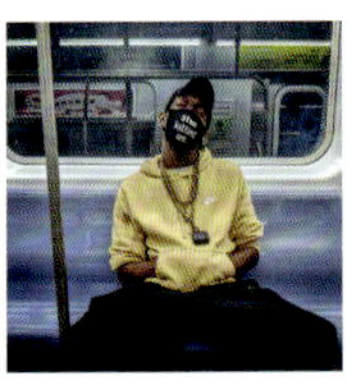

#StopKillingUs
September 2020

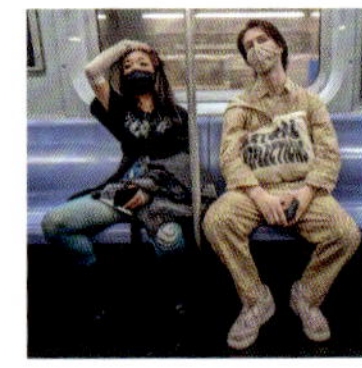

#reflections
October 2021

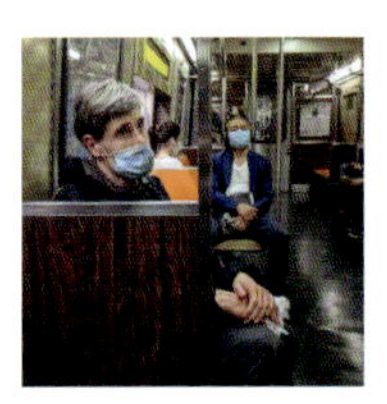

#channelingpaneling
September 2021

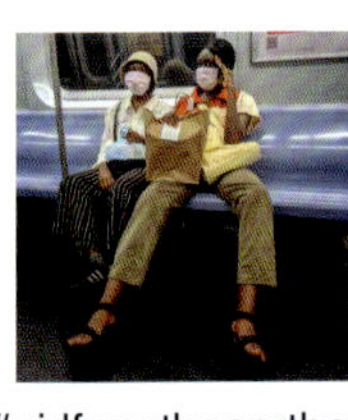

#girlfromthenorthcountry
October 2021

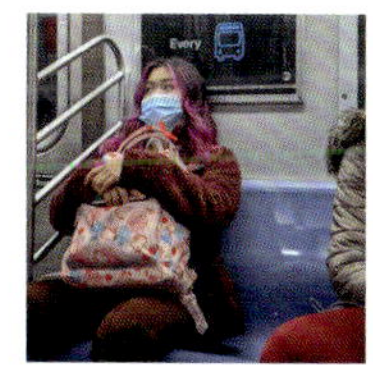

#hellokitty / #every 🚇
January 2022

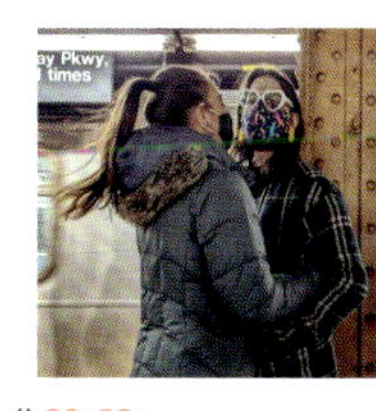

❤️ ❤️
February 2022

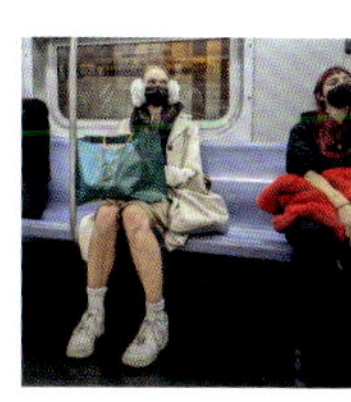

#catch
April 2022

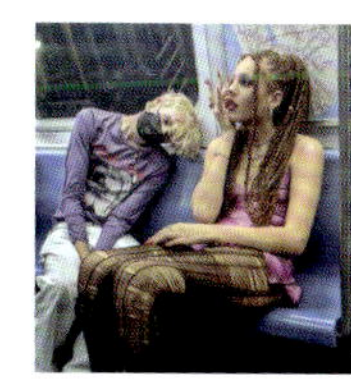

#helloboy
October 2021

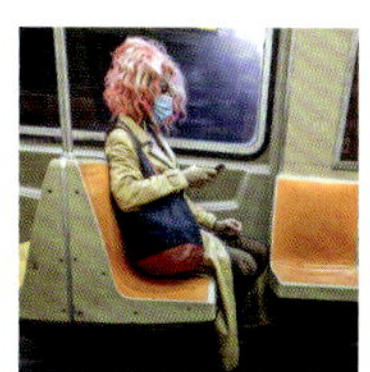

#brightlight
December 2021

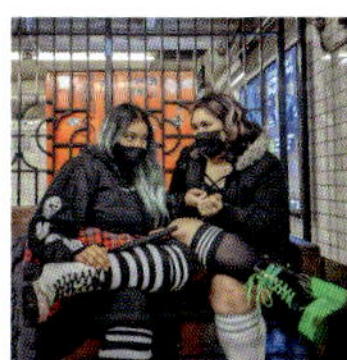

#LetUs
February 2022

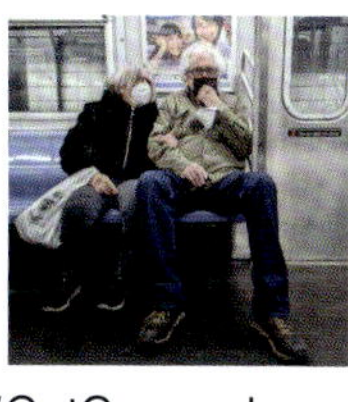

#GetCovered
March 2022

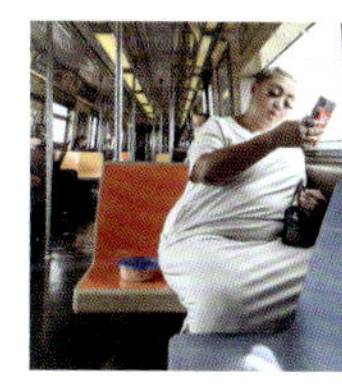

#supreme
October 2021

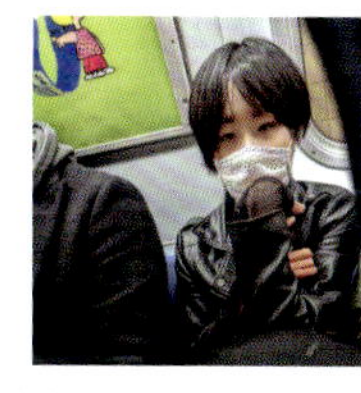

#dots
January 2022

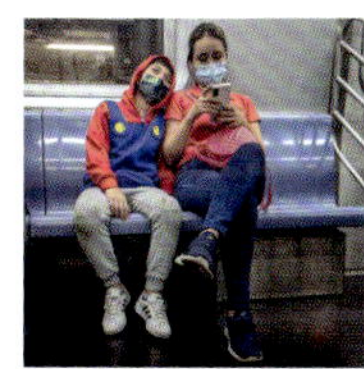

#supermario
April 2022

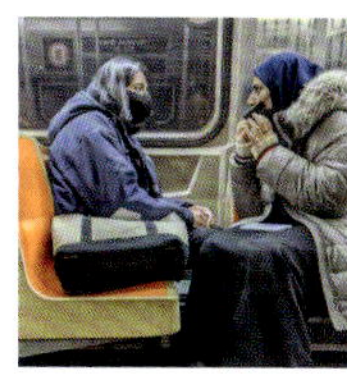

#bronxbound
March 2022

SUBWAYGRAM

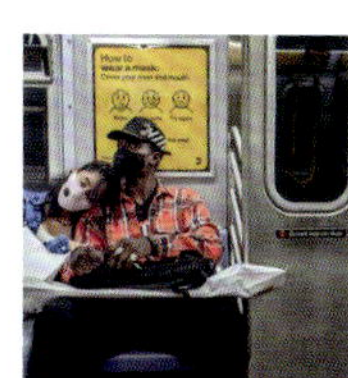

#theone!
November 2021

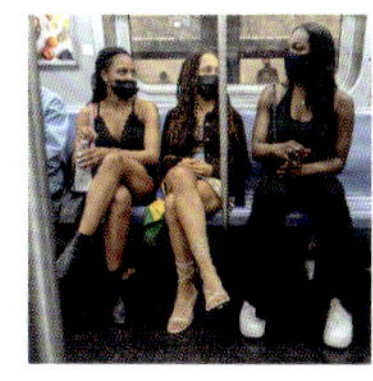

#1
April 2022

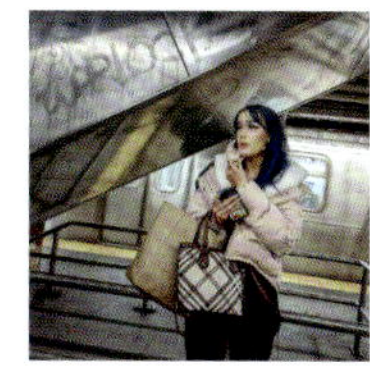

#warlock
December 2021

ACKNOWLEDGMENTS

Dedicated to all of my fellow travelers on the journey, including:

My family, who have inspired me through their strength, courage, and perseverance, especially my mother and father, my grandparents, my brother Ben, my nieces Bailee and Danielle, and my nephew Max.

My friends, who have helped me feel like I belong, helped me figure out all that I'm capable of, and have gotten me back on track when I've lost my way, especially Sean Bruich, Laurence Moore, Andrew Mercando, Leah Delany, Derek Yarbrough, Simone Onnis, Matt Heller, Andrew Martinez-Fonts, James Miller, Andrew Hasserlat, Fred Fang, Allene Jue, Gavin Clark, Christopher Tow, and Mike Osborne.

My teachers, who recognized and helped me hone my photographic vision, including Joel Leivick, Greg Niemeyer, and Jean Marie Casbarian.

The team at Daylight Books, who believed in my potential and encouraged me to tell my own story through this work. Thank you, Michael Itkoff and Ursula Damm.